영어와 삶을 동시에 변화시키는 100일의 여정

하루 10분
영어 필사의 기적 

하루 10분 영어 필사의 기적

초판 1쇄 발행 2026년 1월 6일

지은이 Brett Lindsay
옮긴이 정시윤
펴낸곳 ㈜에스제이더블유인터내셔널
펴낸이 양홍걸 이시원

홈페이지 www.siwonschool.com
주소 서울시 영등포구 영신로 166 시원스쿨
교재 구입 문의 02)2014-8151
고객센터 02)6409-0878

ISBN 979-11-7550-554-4 (13740)
Number 1-010404-30303000-09

하루 10분
영어 필사의 기적

Brett Lindsay 지음

S 시원스쿨닷컴

하루 10분이면 영어 실력도, 삶도
완전히 달라질 수 있습니다.

영어 실력도 높이고 삶도 풍요롭게 만드는 여정에 오신 것을 환영합니다. 저는 Brett Lindsay입니다. 오프라인에서는 SAT(미국 대학 입학시험)를, 온라인에서는 영어를 가르치는 선생으로, 저는 과정에 관련된 내용만이 아니라 학생들 내면에 긍정적인 학습 태도가 자리 잡도록 가르치고 있습니다. 특히, 학생들이 좌절과 도전을 마주할 때, 마음가짐을 바로잡고 더 나은 방식으로 접근하도록 돕습니다. 25년간 수많은 학생을 지도해 온 저는 더 많은 사람이 원하는 삶과 뛰어난 영어 실력을 함께 갖추도록 돕는 것을 목표로 합니다. 그래서 언어 실력을 키우는 동시에 충만한 삶을 이끄는 통찰을 주는 책을 가져왔습니다. 이 책에서 만날 영감을 주는 글 100편은 감사, 역경 극복, 배움, 목표와 꿈, 사랑, 근성, 행복, 성장, 자기 돌봄, 인생 철학이라는 10가지 핵심 주제에 따라 여러분을 인도하여 줄 것입니다.

영어 실력을 키우고 더 나은 삶을 살아가는 데 가장 좋은 방법은 무엇일까요? 저는 단순하지만 강력한 접근 방식을 제안합니다. 매일 10~15분씩, 100일 동안 이 책의 글을 읽어 보세요. 하지만 단순히 읽는 데 그치지 말고, 글 속의 사상에 깊이 빠져들거나, 손으로 써 보거나, 소리 내어 읽어 보세요. 그 지혜가 일상에 스며들어, 여러분은 영어 구사력과 개인적 성장에 변화를 목격하게 될 것입니다.

필사는 다양한 감각을 활용하고 적극적인 참여를 요구하여, 영어 학습 경험을 높이는 강력한 학습 방법입니다. 주로 시각을 사용해 금세 잊어버리게 되는 경우가 많은 수동적인 읽기와는 달리, 필사는 각 단어와 철자, 문장 구조, 문법에 완전히 집중하게 합니다. 이렇게 시각과 청각, 촉각을 수반한 능동적인 연습은 글쓰기 실력을 높이고 영어의 미묘한 뉘앙스를 더 깊이 이해하게 할 뿐 아니라, 어휘와 문법, 생각이 머릿속에 단단히 자리 잡게 도와줍니다. 손으로 직접 쓰는 데 좀 더 시간과 노력을 쏟으면, 글의 교훈과 지혜를 내면화하여 삶에 의미 있게 적용할 가능성이 커집니다. 효과적으로 배우려면 느린 접근 방식이 필요하단 걸 기억하세요. 책의 내용과 깊게 연결될수록 깨달음은 더 오래, 강렬하게 남습니다.

비슷한 주제끼리 묶지 않은 이유가 궁금하실지도 모르겠어요. 그 답은 우리 뇌가 설계된 방식에 있답니다. 배움은 역동적이고 다양할 때 가장 효과적입니다. 간격을 둔 반복은 비슷한 주제가 시간 간격을 두고 되돌아오는 방식입니다. 이렇게 하면 기억에 더 오래 남을 뿐 아니라, 새롭게 배운 내용이 머릿속의 기존 지식과 연결되어, 기억 수용력이 효과적으로 견고해지고 확장됩니다. 이 책은 이 기법을 강화하도록 구성하여, 매일 새로운 주제, 신선한 시각을 불러오도록 했습니다.

이 책은 나이나 직업과 관계없이, 모두를 위한 책입니다. 고등학생이든, 직장인이든, 여유를 즐기는 퇴직자든, 여기 실린 글은 울림을 줄 것입니다. 일상 영어로 구성해, 고등학교 수준의 영어 실력을 지닌 사람들이 쉽게 접근할 수 있고, 제공된 번역은 이해를 도울 것입니다. 더욱이, 이 책은 삶의 모든 단계에 있는 사람들을 지혜로 가득 채워 주는 아주 좋은 선물이 될 것입니다.

본문에 참여하는 데는 두 가지 주요 방식, 즉 필사와 소리 내어 읽기가 있습니다. 다음 장 < 이 책을 활용하는 법 >에서 자세히 이야기할 각각의 방식은 영어 실력을 강화할 뿐 아니라, 각각의 글이 전해 주는 삶의 교훈에 대한 이해를 깊어지게 할 것입니다.

이 여정을 나설 때, 책 속의 생각들을 꼭 받아들이기를 바랍니다. 영감을 받고 도전하세요. 그러면 영어 실력이 향상될 뿐 아니라, 삶과 주변 사람들에게도 긍정적인 변화를 불러올 것이라 자신합니다.

이 빛나는 여정에 행운이 함께하길 바랍니다!

Brett Lindsay

10 minutes a day can totally transform
your English and life

Welcome to a journey that combines the mastery of the English language with the enrichment of life itself. I am Brett Lindsay, and as an in-person SAT teacher and online English teacher, I teach not only the content related to the courses but also establish a positive learning attitude in my students. Specifically, I help them adjust their mindset and change their methods when facing setbacks and challenges. Having guided many students for twenty-five years, I aim to help more people achieve the life they desire and excellent English proficiency. Therefore, I bring to you a book designed not just to enhance your linguistic skills but also to offer insights into leading a fulfilling life. In these pages, you will discover a collection of 100 inspirational articles, each a beacon guiding you through 10 significant themes: gratitude, conquering adversity, learning, goals & dreams, love, grit, happiness, growth, self-care, and philosophy.

What is the best way to both improve your English and lead a better life? I propose a simple yet powerful approach: spend 10-15 minutes each day for 100 days reading an article from this book. But don't just read; immerse yourself in the ideas, transcribe them, or read them out loud. Let the wisdom seep into your daily life and witness the transformation in both your command of English and your personal development.

Transcription is a powerful learning tool that elevates your English learning experience by engaging multiple senses and demanding active participation. Unlike passive reading, which primarily uses your sense of sight and often leads to quick forgetting, transcribing a text requires you to focus intensely on each word, its spelling, sentence structure, and grammar. This active engagement, which involves sight, hearing, and touch, not only enhances your writing skills and deepens your understanding of English nuances but also helps to fix vocabulary, grammar, and ideas firmly in your mind. By investing this extra effort and time in transcription, you are more likely to internalize the lessons and wisdom of the text, allowing you to apply them meaningfully to your life. Remember, effective learning requires a slower approach: engaging deeply with the material ensures a more lasting and impactful understanding.

You might wonder, why not group similar themes together? The answer lies in the way our brains are wired. Learning is most effective when it is dynamic and varied. Spaced repetition is a method where similar topics are revisited after intervals of time. This not only deepens the impression but also connects newly learned content with existing knowledge in the brain, effectively solidifying and expanding memory capacity. This book is structured to leverage this technique, ensuring each day brings a new theme, a fresh perspective.

This book is for everyone, regardless of age or career. Whether you're a high school student, a working professional, or enjoying retirement, these articles will resonate with you. Crafted in everyday English, the language is accessible to people with a senior high school level of proficiency, and the translations provided will aid in understanding. Moreover, this book serves as an ideal gift, brimming with wisdom for individuals at every stage of life.

There are two main methods to engage with the text: transcribing and reading aloud. Each method, thoroughly discussed in the next section, "How to Use This Book," will not only bolster your English skills but also deepen your understanding of the life lessons each article imparts.

As you embark on this journey, I encourage you to embrace the ideas within. Let them inspire and challenge you. If you do, I am confident that not only will your English improve, but you'll also bring positive changes to your life and to those around you.

Wishing you all the best on this enlightening journey!

Brett Lindsay

차례

Phase 1
Embark on Journey of Change 변화의 여정에 올라타기

Phase 2
Establish Objectives 목표 세우기

Phase 3
Launch Action Steps 행동 단계 시작하기

Phase 4
Gradually Advance 서서히 나아가기

Phase 5
Persistently Execute 끈질기게 실행하기

Phase 8

Reflect on Outcomes 결과를 되돌아보기

Phase 9

Consolidate and Stabilize 강화하고 안정시키기

Phase 10

Continually Go Beyond 계속해서 넘어서

이 책을 활용하는 법

영어 원어민이 말로 하고 글로 쓰는 자연스러운 표현

이 책은 원어민들이 일상에서 소통하는 방식을 반영하여 스스럼없는 대화체로 쓰였습니다. 너무 형식적인 학문적 표현은 제외했습니다. 이 선택은 의도적이었습니다. 생활 영어는 말하고 쓸 때 대부분 형식에 얽매이지 않기 때문입니다. 이런 표현을 받아들이면, 원어민이 말하고 쓰는, 자연스러운 영어 표현에 더 가까워질 것입니다.

본문에 참여하기

이 책에서 최대한 이익을 얻으려면 여러 감각을 활용해 본문에 적극적으로 참여해야 합니다. 좋은 학습은 제대로 연습해서 긍정적인 습관으로 발전시키는 것입니다. 읽으면서 정확한 발음을 내 것으로 만드는 걸 목표로 하세요. 발음은 QR 코드로 제공하는 저자가 직접 녹음한 음원을 들으며 강화할 수 있는 기술입니다. 읽으면서 듣는 과정을 통해 무의식적으로 원어민의 발음을 받아들이게 됩니다. 음원은 다양한 방법으로 활용할 수 있습니다. 그 방법에는 발음과 억양, 리듬을 그냥 듣기, 들으면서 조용히 읽기, 재생, 일시 정지를 반복하며 듣기(한 문장을 재생하고, 잠시 멈추고, 그 문장을 소리 내어 읽기), 녹음을 따라 소리 내어 읽기가 있습니다. 저는 지금도 외국어를 연습하는 데 이 효과적인 방식을 활용합니다.

음원에서 들은 제 목소리가 머릿속에 단단히 자리 잡으면, 이제 한 단어 한 단어, 본문을 소리 내어 읽고 손으로 써 보세요. 연필로 쓰면서 음원(단어의 발음과 문장의 억양, 글 전체의 리듬)을 떠올려 보세요. 소리 내어 읽는 동시에 쓰면서, 영어 학습 결과를 깊게 강화해 보세요. 얼마나 많이 해야 하냐고요? 최소 다섯 번, 많이 하면 할수록 좋습니다. 혹시 영어 본문에서 이해되지 않는 부분이 있다면, 한국어 번역을 참고해 전체 의미를 파악해 보세요. 이 글들에 더 많은 시간과 감각을 투자할수록 학습 효과가 더 커진다는 것을 기억하세요.

삶에 적용하기

이상적인 접근 방식은 매일 아침에 일어나자마자 혹은 잠들기 전, 이 책에 일정한 시간에 할애하는 것입니다. 꾸준함이 핵심이죠. 하루가 너무 바쁘다면, 적어도 본문을 듣고 소리 내어 읽어 보세요. 이렇게 하면 습관을 지키고 학습 과정을 활발하게 유지할 수 있습니다.

많은 글에 간단한 일부터 더 전념해야 하는 일에 이르기까지, 실천해 볼 수 있는 단계가 포함되어 있습니다. 어떤 글은 일상 루틴에 쉽게 결합할 수 있는 습관들을 소개하여, 영어 실력을 높일 뿐 아니라 삶도 풍요롭게 합니다.

성장이라는 여정

이 책은 단순히 언어를 공부하는 도구가 아닙니다. 삶의 다양한 단계와 도전을 헤쳐 나가는 여정의 동반자입니다. 책을 따라가며, 마음을 열고 자신의 필요에 맞게 연습 방법을 조율해 보세요. 목표는 100일 동안, 멈추지 않고 이 책을 끝내는 것입니다. 그 후에는, 언제든 다시 돌아와 여러 번 탐색할 수 있습니다. 100일이 끝날 무렵엔 영어 실력은 물론, 삶을 바라보는 관점까지 대단히 풍요로워져 있을 것입니다. 하루하루 나아가는 배움과 성장의 여정을 기원합니다.

How to Use This Book

The Natural Style of Speaking and Writing of Native English Speakers

This book is written in an informal, conversational English that mirrors how native speakers communicate in everyday scenarios, except for very formal academic settings. This choice is deliberate, as real-life English is mostly informal, both in speech and writing. By embracing this style, you'll find yourself closer to the natural style of English as it is spoken and written by native speakers.

Engaging with the Text

Maximizing the benefits from this book requires active engagement with the texts, using multiple senses. Good learning involves practicing correctly to develop positive habits. As you read, aim to internalize good pronunciation, a skill you can enhance by listening to my recordings of the passages (accessible via QR code). This process of listening while reading ensures that you subconsciously adopt native-speaker pronunciation. You can engage with the audio in various ways: passive listening for pronunciation, intonation, and rhythm; simultaneously listening and reading silently; play and pause listening (play a sentence, pause, and read the sentence out loud); or reading aloud following the audio. Btw, I still use this fantastic method to practice foreign languages.

Once you've got my voice firmly in your mind, you should read the text aloud and write it down, word for word. Write down the text with a pencil, recalling the sound of the audio recording (the pronunciation of the words, the intonation of the sentences, and the rhythm of the entire passage). Read aloud and write simultaneously to deeply consolidate the results of your English learning. How many times should you do this? At least five times, the more the better. By the way, if there are parts of the English text you don't understand, you can refer to the Korean translation to help you understand the overall article. Remember: the more time and sensory engagement you invest in these passages, the more effective your learning will be.

Fitting It into Your Life

The ideal approach is to dedicate a specific time each day to this book, either just after waking up or before going to bed. Consistency is key. If a day gets too busy, at least listen to and read the article out loud. This maintains your habit and keeps the learning process active.

Many articles include actionable steps, ranging from the simple to those requiring more dedication. Some introduce habits that can be easily integrated into your daily routine, not only enhancing your English but also enriching your life.

A Journey of Growth

This book isn't just a tool to learn language; it's a companion on your journey through life's various stages and challenges. As you progress, remember to keep an open mind and adapt the exercises to suit your needs. Your goal is to complete the book in 100 days, without stopping. Afterward, you can always revisit and explore it multiple times. By the end of these 100 days, you'll find not only your English, but also your perspective on life, profoundly enriched. Here's to a journey of learning and growth, one day at a time.

Embark on Journey of Change

변화의 여정에 올라타기

"When you start appreciating what you have,
instead of lamenting what you don't have,
something shifts."
-from Day 1-

"가지지 못한 걸 아쉬워하는 대신
가진 것에 감사하기 시작하면 무언가 달라져."

The Secret to Feeling Rich.

Gratitude is like a magical lens that changes how you see things. When you start appreciating what you have, instead of lamenting what you don't have, something shifts. It's like suddenly, what you have multiplies in value. It's not about having a lot—it's about appreciating what you have. That's the secret to feeling truly rich.

So, even on tough days, finding something, no matter how small, to be thankful for, can change the way you view life. It's about realizing that even the simplest things can bring joy, and in recognizing that, you find contentment. It's really an awesome way to live.

●●●

풍요롭게 느끼는 비결

감사는 세상을 바라보는 방식을 변화시키는 마법 렌즈 같아. 가지지 못한 걸 아쉬워하는 대신 가진 것에 감사하기 시작하면 무언가 달라져. 갑자기 가진 것의 가치가 배가 되는 것처럼 말이야. 중요한 건 많이 갖는 게 아니야, 가진 것에 감사하는 거야. 그게 진정으로 풍요롭게 느끼는 비결이야.

그래서 힘든 날에도 아주 작은 거라도 상관없이 감사할 것을 찾으면, 삶을 바라보는 방식이 달라져. 지극히 평범한 것도 기쁨을 불러올 수 있음을 깨닫고, 이를 깨달음으로써 만족을 얻게 돼. 삶을 살아가는 정말 멋진 방식이지.

lament 아쉬워하다, 한탄하다 | shift 바뀌다 | multiply 증가시키다, 곱하다 |
realize 깨닫다, 이해하다 | contentment 만족

Laugh Away Life's Burdens.

You ever notice how sometimes life seems too heavy? Next time you're in a funk, try this—just laugh. Go watch something funny, such as a movie or sitcom, or hang out with that friend who cracks you up.

You know why? Laughter's like this magical stress buster. When you laugh, your brain releases these feel-good chemicals, and suddenly the weight on your shoulders feels lighter.

I'm not saying laughter's going to solve all your problems, but it's gonna make them a whole lot easier to tackle. So, go ahead, give yourself a break and let loose a few laughs. You'll feel more relaxed, and who knows, the answer you've been looking for might just pop into your head.

●●●

삶의 짐을 웃어넘기기

때로 삶이 너무 무겁게 느껴질 때 있지? 다음에 우울한 기분이 들면 이렇게 해 봐. 그냥 웃어 봐. 영화나 시트콤처럼 재미있는 걸 보거나, 너를 마구 웃게 해 주는 친구를 만나 봐.

왜인지 알아? 웃음은 마법 같은 스트레스 해소법이거든. 웃으면 뇌는 기분을 좋게 하는 화학 물질을 내뿜어서, 순식간에 어깨에 얹힌 무게가 가볍게 느껴져.

웃는다고 모든 문제가 해결되지는 않겠지만, 그 문제들과 맞붙는 게 훨씬 더 쉬워질 거야. 그러니 그냥 한숨 돌리고 조금 웃어 봐. 더 편안해져서 찾고 있던 답이 머릿속에 불쑥 떠오를지도 몰라.

DATE _____ / _____ / _____

funk 우울, 두려움, 걱정 | sitcom 시트콤 |
stress buster 스트레스 해소법 | release 방출하다, 내뿜다

Practice Doesn't Necessarily Make Perfect!

Does "practice make perfect?" Not quite! Practice makes permanent, but only perfect practice makes perfect. Keep that in mind when you're honing your skills.

Don't fall into the trap of mindless repetition, as that might just reinforce bad habits. Make sure you're always fully engaged and mindful in your practice, aiming for improvement each time.

And hey, this rule applies to copying texts from this book as well! Focus on your actions and work toward excellence. That way, you'll not only improve but also build a strong foundation for future success. Always remember, the quality of your practice is just as important as, if not more than, the quantity.

•••

연습한다고 반드시 완벽해지지는 않아!

'연습하면 완벽해질까?' 꼭 그렇진 않아! 연습하면 습관이 되기는 하지만, 완벽을 만드는 건 완벽한 연습뿐이야. 기술을 연마할 땐 꼭 명심해.

무의식적으로 반복하는 함정에 빠지지 마. 오히려 나쁜 습관만 강화할 수도 있거든. 연습할 땐 항상 온전히 집중하고 의식해서, 매 순간 앞으로 나아가는 걸 목표로 하도록 해.

그리고 이 원칙을 이 책 본문을 따라 쓰는 데도 적용해 봐! 행동에 집중하면서 최고를 향해 가는 거야. 그러면 실력이 향상될 뿐 아니라 미래의 성공을 이끌 단단한 기반도 쌓을 수 있어. 항상 기억해, 연습의 양도 중요하지만, 질은 그보다 더 중요하다는 걸.

permanent 영구적인, 고정적인 | trap 함정 | hone 연마하다 |
reinforce 강화하다 | fully engaged 완전히 집중하다

The Definition of Insanity.

Albert Einstein once said, "The definition of insanity is doing the same thing over and over again and expecting different results." When you've been doing something for quite a while, such as trying to figure out a math problem, but you're not making any progress, you may have fallen into this trap.

The most important thing you can do is to stop what you've been doing and try a different method. Even if the new method doesn't work, it will at least give you a new angle on the problem and may give you a new idea you can use to solve it.

Keep changing your approach and eventually, you'll find a method that works.

So, remember: if one approach isn't working, take another approach.

미친 짓의 정의

알베르트 아인슈타인은 '미친 짓의 정의는 같은 행동을 반복하면서 다른 결과를 기대하는 것'이라고 말했어. 수학 문제를 풀려고 애쓰는 등, 어떤 일을 오랫동안 해 왔는데도 전혀 진척이 없다면 이 함정에 빠진 건지도 몰라.

이때 해 볼 수 있는 가장 중요한 일은 지금껏 하던 걸 멈추고 다른 방식을 시도해 보는 거야. 새로운 방식이 효과가 없더라도, 적어도 그 문제를 새로운 각도로 보게 될 거야. 어쩌면 문제를 푸는 데 활용할 수 있는 새로운 아이디어를 가져다줄지도 몰라.

계속 접근 방식을 바꾸다 보면 결국 효과가 있는 방식을 찾게 될 거야.

그러니 기억해. 어떤 방식이 통하지 않는다면 다른 방식을 써 봐.

definition 정의 | insanity 미친 짓, 정신 이상 |
angle 각도, 관점 | approach 접근 방식

Don't Let Your Love Disappear Faster Than an Ice Cream on a Hot Day.

Hey, let's be real. In daily life, it's so easy to forget what made you fall head over heels for your partner in the first place.

But here's the deal—really noticing their great qualities is the secret to keeping the love alive. If you let yourself focus on what annoys you, well, you'll see your affection disappear faster than an ice cream on a hot day.

So, here's your takeaway: actively appreciating what makes your lover awesome is like a golden ticket to a happier relationship. It's like falling in love over and over again. Do it regularly and you're not just maintaining love, you're increasing that love.

● ● ●

사랑이 더운 날 아이스크림보다 더 빨리 사라지게 내버려두지 마.

자, 현실적으로 생각해 보자. 일상을 살다 보면 처음 연인에게 푹 빠진 이유를 잊어버리기가 너무 쉬워.

하지만 중요한 건 이거야. 그 사람의 멋진 면을 알아보는 게 사랑이 계속 살아 숨 쉬게 하는 비결이야. 짜증 나는 부분에 초점을 맞추면, 글쎄, 애정이 더운 날 아이스크림보다 더 빨리 사라지는 모습을 보게 될 거야.

그러니 꼭 기억해. 연인을 근사하게 하는 점을 적극적으로 알아보는 것이야말로 더 행복한 관계로 가는 황금 티켓이나 다름없어. 마치 몇 번이고 다시 사랑에 빠지는 것과 같아. 그렇게 꾸준히 하면 사랑은 지속될 뿐 아니라 점점 더 깊어질 거야.

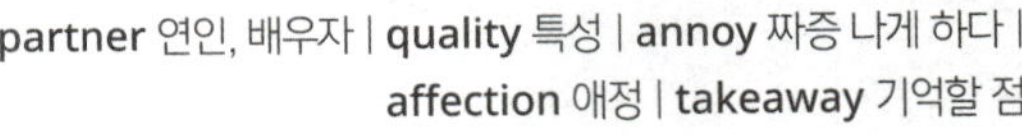

partner 연인, 배우자 | quality 특성 | annoy 짜증 나게 하다 |
affection 애정 | takeaway 기억할 점

How Do You Eat an Elephant?

There's an old saying, "How do you eat an elephant?", to which the answer is "One bite at a time." Got a big goal? Awesome! Slice it into bite-sized pieces. These little chunks are your milestones. It's much easier for you to believe you can achieve these smaller goals, which gives you more motivation to do the necessary work to achieve them.

And here's another key: every time you tick something off your list, give yourself a pat on the back. It could be a treat, a break, or a bounce on a rebounder—whatever gets you pumped. This isn't just about making progress, either: it's about enjoying the journey, you know?

On the other hand, why do most people quit? They set huge, unrealistic goals and think, "I'll never achieve them!" So, set small, doable goals, reward yourself, and keep going! Your persistence is going to pay off, step by victorious step!

●●●

코끼리를 어떻게 먹을까?

'코끼리를 어떻게 먹을까?'라는 말이 있어. 그 답은 '한 번에 한입씩'이야. 큰 목표가 있어? 좋아! 그걸 한입 크기로 잘라 봐. 이 작은 조각들이 네 이정표야. 이런 작은 목표라면 이룰 수 있다고 믿기가 훨씬 쉽고, 그 믿음은 목표를 이루는 데 필요한 일을 해낼 동기를 더 많이 부여해 줘.

그리고 핵심이 하나 더 있어. 목록을 하나씩 지워 나갈 때마다 스스로 칭찬해 주는 거야. 선물이든 휴식이든 트램펄린에서 방방 뛰는 거든, 신나는 거라면 뭐든 좋아. 중요한 건 그냥 진도를 나가는 게 아니라 그 여정을 즐기는 거야, 알겠지?

한편으로, 왜 대부분 사람이 중간에 그만둘까? 거대하고 비현실적인 목표를 세우고 '절대 해내지 못할 거야!'라고 생각하기 때문이야. 그러니 작고 실행 가능한 목표를 정하고, 자신에게 보상하며 계속 나아가! 끈기는 보답받을 거야, 승리의 한 걸음, 한 걸음으로!

chunk 조각, 덩어리 | milestone 이정표 | treat 대접, 선물 |
rebounder 소형 트램펄린 | doable 할 수 있는

Started Questioning the Meaning of Life?

Ever get so tired that you start questioning the meaning of life and find everybody irritating? When you're brimming with resentment, hate life, and are constantly venting, you really need to take a break from work or studies and just get some good sleep.

Here's how: First, sleep in a cool, dark room. Also, gradually train your circadian rhythm. This means keeping the same sleeping schedule, even on weekends: go to bed at the same time each night and wake up at the same time.

Now, here's a toughie: If you must drink coffee or tea, finish drinking it by 2pm so most of the caffeine is out of your system before bed. If you do all of these things, you'll feel so much more energetic and happier you won't believe it. You'll also be able to think more clearly and deal with difficult problems with ease. Just do it!

●●●

삶의 의미가 의심되기 시작했어?

너무 지쳐서 삶의 의미에 의문이 들기 시작하고 모두가 거슬릴 때 있지? 분노가 머리끝까지 차오르고 인생이 싫고 끊임없이 분통이 터질 때, 그럴 땐 일이나 공부를 잠시 멈추고 그냥 푹 자야 해.

방법은, 우선 쾌적하고 어두운 곳에서 자는 거야. 그리고 서서히 생체 리듬을 다스려 보는 거지. 취침 시간을 똑같이 유지하라는 뜻이야. 주말에도 마찬가지야. 매일 같은 시간에 자고 같은 시간에 일어나. 자, 어려운 일 하나. 커피나 차를 마셔야 한다면 오후 2시 전까지 마셔서 잠자리에 들기 전에 카페인 대부분이 몸에서 빠져나가게 해.

이런 원칙들을 다 지키면 훨씬 더 활력이 넘치고 믿기지 않을 만큼 기분이 좋아질 거야. 또한 더 명확하게 사고하고 어려운 문제들을 수월하게 풀 수 있게 될 거야. 그냥 해 봐!

irritating 거슬리는 | brim with 넘치도록 차다 | resentment 분노, 원망 |
vent 분통을 터뜨리다 | toughie 어려운 일

Make Intelligent Choices Every Day.

Life's full of not-so-comfy spots. Whether you're stuck doing something or pushing yourself to grow, you're going to feel a bit uncomfortable either way. Now, here's the amazing thing. Not all discomfort is equal.

Take discipline, for example. It's like a little nudge every day, a tiny bit of unease that helps you get closer to your dreams. It's like having a small stone in your shoe on a long, rewarding hike.

On the other hand, there's failure. It's like falling flat on your face in front of a crowd—ouch, some serious unease that can really hurt. So, it's kinda like choosing between a small, daily stone or a big, painful fall. Discipline is your daily little stone, while failure is that big nasty fall waiting to happen if you're not careful.

So, when it comes to feeling uneasy, pick the small nudge of discipline over the big pain of failure. It's your choice every day. Choose smart!

●●●

매일 똑똑한 선택을 해.

삶은 그다지 편치 않은 지점으로 가득해. 어떤 일에 발이 묶여 있든, 성장하려고 자신을 밀어붙이고 있든, 어느 쪽으로든 조금 불편할 거야. 그런데 놀라운 사실이 있어. 불편함이 모두 똑같지는 않다는 거야.

자기 훈련을 예로 들어 보자. 그건 마치 매일 등을 살짝 떠미는 느낌으로, 꿈에 더 가까이 다가가게 도와주는 자그마한 불편함이야. 길지만 보람 있는 등산길에서 신발에 들어간 작은 돌멩이 같은 거지.

반면, 실패는 사람들 앞에서 얼굴부터 넘어지는 것과 같아. 아야, 정말 아플 수도 있는 심각한 불편함이지. 그러니까 작은 일상의 돌멩이와 크고 아프게 넘어지는 일 중에서 하나를 고르는 것과 비슷해. 훈련은 일상에서 부딪히는 작은 돌멩이고, 실패는 조심하지 않으면 결국 겪게 되는 크고 끔찍한 추락이야.

그러니 꼭 불편함을 느껴야 한다면 실패라는 커다란 고통 말고 훈련이라는 등 떠밀림을 골라. 매일 해야 하는 선택이야. 현명하게 선택해!

spot 지점 | discipline 훈련, 훈육 | unease 불편 | pick 고르다

Plant Seeds of Positivity for Yourself.

Starting and ending your day with positive thoughts is like nourishing your mind. It fills your day with confidence and good energy. It's a simple yet impactful way to remember your worth.

Try this: when you wake up and before you sleep, think of good things about yourself. Maybe tell yourself, "I like myself," "I feel terrific," or "I am a great friend and people appreciate me."

This habit is like planting seeds of positivity that grow all day. Doing it regularly helps shape a confident and upbeat mindset. The way you talk to yourself really shapes your day. Lift yourself up each morning and night—it makes a big difference in keeping the positivity flowing!

●●●

자신에게 긍정이라는 씨앗을 심어 줘.

긍정적인 생각으로 하루를 시작하고 끝내는 건 마음에 영양분을 주는 일과 같아. 자신감과 좋은 에너지로 하루를 채워 주지. 자기 가치를 기억하는, 단순하지만 강력한 방식이야.

이렇게 해 봐. 아침에 눈을 뜰 때, 그리고 잠들기 전에 자신의 좋은 점들을 떠올려 봐. '난 내가 좋아', '나 좀 멋진데', '난 아주 좋은 친구고, 사람들은 내 진가를 알아'라고 스스로 말해 봐.

이런 습관은 하루 종일 자라나는 긍정의 씨앗을 심는 거나 다름없어. 꾸준히 하다 보면 자신감 있고 낙관적인 마음가짐을 만드는 데 도움이 돼. 자신에게 말하는 방식이 실제로 하루를 결정지어. 매일 아침과 밤에 스스로 기운을 북돋아 줘. 긍정적인 흐름을 이어 가는 데 커다란 차이를 낳을 거야!

nourish 영양분을 주다 | impactful 강력한, 매우 효과적인 |
shape 만들다, 정하다 | upbeat 낙관적인

Pay Attention to the Words You Habitually Use.

A word of caution: select your words wisely.

There are so many ways to describe something, and each one will alter how you feel about it. For example, if you lose your wallet, you probably won't be too happy about it. Imagine telling your friend, "I'm so angry I could tear somebody to shreds!" That would make you angrier than you originally were. Imagine instead that you said, "I'm a little upset about it." You wouldn't feel as bad, would you? So, use less intense words when things upset you.

On the other hand, you can use this technique for positive things, too. If you had some great pasta, you could say, "That penne was out of this world!" You'd feel even better than if you had said, "That penne was pretty good." This holds true for any language you're using, too.

Remember, the stronger your language, the stronger you feel. Therefore, you should be very careful with the words you habitually use.

●●●

습관적으로 쓰는 단어에 주의를 기울여 봐.

주의 사항: 단어를 신중하게 골라.

무언가를 표현하는 방법은 아주 많고, 그에 따라 느끼는 감정도 달라져. 예를 들어, 지갑을 잃어버린다면 아마 기분이 좋지는 않을 거야. 그래서 친구에게 '너무 화가 나서 누굴 찢어발길 수 있을 정도야!'라고 말한다고 상상해 봐. 그렇게 하면 원래보다 더 화가 날 거야. 대신, '조금 속상하네'라고 말한다고 상상해 봐. 그렇게 기분 나쁘지 않겠지? 그러니 화나는 일이 있을 땐 덜 격한 단어를 써 봐.

반면, 이 기술은 긍정적인 상황에도 활용할 수 있어. 맛있는 파스타를 먹었다면 '그 펜네 파스타 기가 막혔어!'라고 말할 수 있어. '그 펜네 파스타 꽤 맛있었어'라고 말했을 때보다 더 기분 좋아질 거야. 이건 네가 쓰고 있는 어떤 언어에도 유효해.

기억해, 말이 강할수록 감정도 강해진다는 걸. 그러니까 습관적으로 사용하는 단어들에 아주 주의를 기울여야 해.

caution 주의, 경고 | alter 바꾸다 | intense 격한 |
habitually 습관적으로

Phase

2

Establish Objectives

목표 세우기

"So don't exhaust yourself chasing after
perfection; instead aim for improvement."
-from Day 18-

"그러니 완벽을 좇느라 스스로를 지치게 하지 말고,
대신 나아지는 것을 목표로 해."

Kickstart the Day with Gratitude.

Here's a cool little trick to start your day off on the right foot. When you're sipping your morning coffee or tea, think of three different things you're thankful for. And try to mix it up every day. It could be as simple as the sun shining, a good book you're reading, or even that new song that gets you pumped. Doing this gets your brain thinking positively and can make the whole day feel brighter.

Plus, it's a moment just for you before the day's hustle kicks in. Give it a try, and you might just notice how even the regular days start to feel a bit more special.

•••

감사로 하루를 시작해 봐.

하루를 기분 좋게 시작하는 작고 멋진 비결이 있어. 아침에 커피나 차를 홀짝이며 고마운 세 가지를 떠올려 보는 거야. 매일 바꾸면서 해 봐. 반짝이는 햇살, 읽고 있는 좋은 책, 마음을 설레게 하는 새로 나온 노래처럼 사소한 것도 좋아. 이렇게 하면 뇌가 긍정적으로 생각하게 되고, 그날 하루가 더 환하게 느껴질 거야.

게다가 이건 그날의 분주함이 시작되기 전, 오롯이 너만을 위한 시간이야. 한번 해 봐, 그러면 평범한 날들조차 조금 더 특별하게 느껴지는 걸 알아챌지도 몰라.

trick 비결, 요령 | sip 홀짝이다 | pumped 신나는 |
hustle 분주함, 소동 | kick in 시작하다

Change the Way You Talk to Yourself.

Listen, life throws curveballs, right? So, here's a cool way to deal with tough times: change how you talk to yourself about them. Instead of going, "Ugh, why me?", switch it to, "Okay, what can I learn here?"

It sounds simple, but trust me, it's powerful. You go from being a victim to being like a detective, figuring stuff out. You stop feeling stuck and start looking for answers or new ways to do things. It's all about the mindset.

So, the next time something tough comes up, don't just complain. Ask yourself how you can grow from it. Makes the challenge kinda exciting, doesn't it?

●●●

자신에게 말하는 방식을 바꿔 봐.

들어 봐, 삶이 예상치 못한 일을 던져 주기도 하잖아, 그렇지? 그래서 여기, 힘든 시간에 대처하는 근사한 방법이 있어. 그 일에 대해 스스로에게 말하는 방식을 바꾸는 거야. '아, 왜 하필 나야?'라고 하는 대신, '좋아, 여기서 배울 수 있는 건 뭐지?'로 바꿔 봐.

단순하게 들리겠지만, 날 믿어 봐, 강력한 방법이니까. 피해자로만 남지 말고 형사처럼 문제를 파헤치는 거야. 막막한 기분을 걷어 내고 해답이나 새로운 방법들을 찾기 시작하는 거지. 모두 마음가짐에 달렸어.

그러니 다음번에 힘든 일이 닥치면 그저 불평만 하지는 마. 그로써 어떻게 성장할 수 있을지 스스로에게 물어봐. 그러면 그 도전이 꽤 신나지 않겠어?

DATE _______ / _______ / ______

음원 바로 듣기

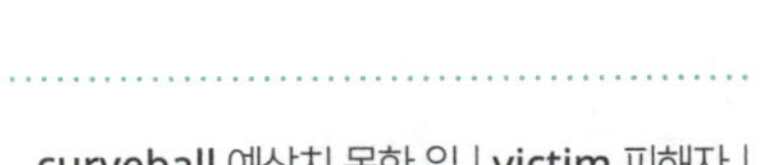
curveball 예상치 못한 일 | victim 피해자 |
detective 형사 | mindset 마음가짐

The Better the Vocabulary, the Higher the Income.

Let's talk about the power of words. Each new word learned correctly opens up opportunities and helps you express yourself better.

And here's something interesting—studies have shown that the better your vocabulary is, the higher your income will be. But there's more. When you have a strong vocabulary, you're able to explain your thoughts more clearly and confidently. People subconsciously judge us by the way we speak and write, and a good vocabulary makes a positive impression. So, make it a habit to learn how to correctly use new words daily and use them in your conversations and writing.

And what's the best way to do this? It's simple. Use the example sentences in the dictionary as templates and substitute one or two of those words with one or two of your own words. Of course, you need to keep the word you want to master in the new sentence. Also, keep the parts of speech the same. Say your sentence out loud 5 times, and you will have learned the word!

●●●

어휘력이 좋을수록 수입도 높아져.

단어의 힘에 대해 이야기해 보자. 제대로 익힌 새로운 단어 하나하나가 기회를 열어 주고 자신을 더 잘 표현하게 도와줘.

그리고 흥미로운 사실이 있어. 연구에 따르면 어휘력이 좋을수록 수입이 높다고 해. 그런데 그게 다가 아니야. 어휘력이 탄탄하면 자기 생각을 더 명확하고 자신 있게 설명할 수 있어. 사람들은 무의식적으로 우리가 말하고 글을 쓰는 방식으로 우리를 판단하거든. 그리고 좋은 어휘력은 긍정적인 인상을 줘. 그러니 매일 새로운 단어들을 정확히 사용하는 방법을 익혀서 대화하고 글을 쓸 때 활용하는 습관을 들여 봐.

이렇게 하는 가장 좋은 방법은 뭘까? 그건 간단해. 사전의 예문을 본보기로 삼아, 예문의 단어 한두 가지를 자신만의 단어 한두 가지로 바꿔 보는 거야. 물론 이때 새 문장에는 네가 익히고 싶은 단어를 넣어야 해. 품사도 똑같이 유지하도록 해. 그 문장을 다섯 번 소리 내어 말하고 나면, 그 단어를 체득하게 될 거야!.

subconsciously 무의식적으로 | judge 판단하다 | template 본보기 |
substitute 바꾸다, 교체하다 | part of speech 품사

Don't Just Set Attainment Goals.

Attainment goals are objectives you set to accomplish specific things, such as obtaining a gold TOEIC certificate or increasing your salary at work. These goals are great, and you should set a completion date for them.

However, in some cases, you should not set attainment goals. Instead, you should set action goals, which are goals about how much time you should spend doing something. Let's use reading an English novel as an example. While this is one of the best ways to improve your English, it is usually a mistake to set the goal of reading a certain number of chapters every day or finishing the novel in a certain number of months. That will only stress you out, and you could easily give up.

Rather, set an action goal: decide to read the novel a certain number of minutes each day and don't worry about how many pages you read. Remain flexible with your goal, too. You may need to decrease the time on some days, and you may want to increase it on others. Do this, and in a few months, you'll be amazed by how much you've achieved!

●●●

성과 목표만 세우지는 마.

성과 목표는 고득점 토익 성적 증명서를 따거나 직장에서 급여를 인상받는 등, 특정한 것을 이루려고 세우는 목표야. 이런 목표는 아주 훌륭해. 목표 달성 날짜를 정해 두면 더 좋지.

하지만 어떤 경우에는 성과 목표를 세우지 말아야 해. 그 대신, 무언가를 하는 데 얼마나 시간을 보낼지, 행동 목표를 정해야 해. 영문 소설 읽기를 예로 들어 보자. 영어 실력을 향상하기에 가장 좋은 방법 중 하나지만, 보통은 매일 몇 장을 읽겠다거나, 몇 달 안에 그 소설을 끝낸다는 목표를 세우는 실수를 하게 돼. 그러면 스트레스만 받고 쉽게 포기할 수도 있어.

그보다 행동 목표를 세워 봐. 매일 몇 분씩 읽기로 하고, 몇 페이지를 읽었는지는 신경 쓰지 않는 거야. 목표도 유연하게 남겨 둬. 어떤 날은 시간을 줄여야 할 수도 있고, 어떤 날은 늘리고 싶을 수도 있어. 이렇게 하면 몇 달 후에는 스스로 얼마나 많이 해냈는지 깜짝 놀랄 거야.

attainment 성과 | obtain 따다, 획득하다 |
a certain number of 일정한 수의 | remain 남다, 머무르다

Love Isn't Just Chemistry.

True love is often mistaken as an emotion, like the butterflies in your stomach, or that chemistry when you first meet someone. While all these feelings are beautiful and thrilling, they are just the tip of the iceberg.

True love goes beyond short-lived emotions; it's about the commitment to stick together, even when the going gets tough. It's about choosing each other every day, even when the butterflies have quieted down. It's the promise to stand by each other, to grow together, to work through the difficulties, and to share life's joys and challenges.

Love matures over time, and the real essence of love is in the willingness to walk the journey together, no matter what. So, when you say you love someone, it's a promise of your loyalty, patience, understanding, and undying support.

•••

사랑은 단지 화학 반응만은 아니야.

진정한 사랑은 종종 설레는 느낌 같은 감정이나 누군가를 처음 만날 때의 화학 반응으로 오해받아. 이런 감정은 모두 아름답고 벅차지만, 빙산의 일각에 불과해.

진정한 사랑은 잠시 스쳐 가는 감정을 넘어, 상황이 힘들 때도 함께하겠다는 약속이야. 설렘이 사그라져도 매일 서로를 선택하는 거지. 서로의 곁을 지키고, 함께 성장하고, 어려움을 헤쳐 나가며, 삶의 기쁨과 도전을 나누겠다는 약속이야.

사랑은 시간이 흐르며 성숙해져. 그리고 그런 사랑의 진정한 본질은 무슨 일이 있어도 그 여정을 함께하겠다는 의지에 있어. 그래서 누군가를 사랑한다고 말할 때는 충실과 인내, 이해, 변치 않는 지지를 약속하는 거야.

음원 바로 듣기

Don't Step out of Your Comfort Zone—Stretch Your Comfort Zone.

You know how we sometimes shy away from things that don't come naturally to us? Let's turn that around. Picture your comfort zone as having an elastic band wrapped around it. You want to keep pushing on that band, stretching it outward so that your comfort zone eventually becomes larger.

Specifically, how about setting aside a bit of time each week, maybe an hour or so, just to work on something that's a bit of a stretch for you? It could be anything that you feel you're not ace at right now. This isn't about becoming perfect at it overnight but about getting comfortable with being uncomfortable and gradually expanding your comfort zone, you know?

Each session, you're stretching your comfort zone, increasing the number of things you can do comfortably. And before you know it, what was once a tough nut to crack starts to feel like second nature. That's how you grow—bit by bit, week by week!

●●●

심리적 안전지대에서 나오지 마. 그 안전지대를 늘려 봐.

우리는 때때로 우리에게 쉽지 않은 일을 피하려고 하잖아? 그걸 한번 뒤집어 보자. 심리적 안전지대에 고무줄이 감겨 있다고 상상해 봐. 그 줄을 계속 밀어내고 바깥쪽으로 늘여서 결국 그 안전지대가 더 커지게 하고 싶을 거야.

매주 얼마의 시간, 한 시간쯤을 따로 떼어, 조금 어려운 일을 해 보는 건 어때? 바로 지금, 썩 잘하지 못한다고 생각되는 어떤 일이든 좋아. 중요한 건 하루아침에 완벽해지는 게 아니라 불편함에 편안해지고 심리적 안전지대를 서서히 넓히는 거야, 알겠지?

매번 심리적 안전지대를 늘리면서, 편안하게 할 수 있는 일들을 늘리는 거야. 그러다 어느 순간, 이전엔 만만치 않던 일이 제2의 천성처럼 느껴지기 시작할 거야. 그게 성장하는 방식이야, 조금씩, 매주!

shy away from ~에서 피하다 | set aside 따로 떼어 두다 |
session 시간, 기간 | a tough nut to crack 만만치 않은, 어려운

Make Hours Feel Like Minutes.

Let's get into something big—discovering what really excites you. It's crucial to do things that spark your interest and make hours feel like minutes. When you dive into something you love, it adds a special kind of joy to your life.

It's possible that you still haven't discovered what you truly love doing, though. So, why not try out new hobbies and activities? Keep an eye out for what gets you really enthusiastic. It might be art, music, writing, reading English novels, or something totally unique to you.

The main thing is to find what grabs you, something that you can get totally wrapped up in. Finding your passion isn't just nice, it can seriously boost your mood and overall happiness. So, what are you waiting for? Get out there and see what you can find!

•••

몇 시간을 몇 분처럼 느껴 봐.

엄청난 걸 시작해 보자. 정말 설레는 게 뭔지 찾아보는 거야. 흥미에 불을 붙이고 몇 시간이 몇 분처럼 느껴지는 일을 해 보는 건 아주 중요해. 좋아하는 일에 뛰어들 때 삶에는 특별한 기쁨이 더해지거든.

진심으로 좋아하는 걸 아직 찾지 못했을지도 몰라. 그렇다면 새로운 취미나 활동을 해 보는 건 어때? 정말 열중할 만한 걸 찾아봐. 미술이나 음악, 글쓰기, 영문 소설 읽기나, 네게는 완전히 독특한 무언가일 수도 있어.

중요한 건 마음을 사로잡는, 완전히 푹 빠질 수 있는 일을 찾아내는 거야. 열정을 찾는 건 그냥 좋은 일이 아니라 기분과 전반적인 행복감을 확 끌어올려 줘. 뭘 기다려? 밖으로 뛰쳐나가 뭘 찾을 수 있는지 확인해 봐.

crucial 중대한 | enthusiastic 열렬한, 열중한 |
grab 사로잡다 | passion 열정

Don't Exhaust Yourself Chasing After Perfection.

You know, perfection is like a mirage. It seems real from a distance, but the closer you get, the more it moves away. It's like climbing a mountain and thinking you've reached the peak, only to find there's yet another peak hiding behind it.

The beauty lies in the climb itself, the process of discovering new views, overcoming challenges, and becoming stronger with each step. That's what improvement is all about. It's not about reaching a point of perfection, but about growing, evolving, and getting better each day.

So, don't exhaust yourself chasing after perfection; instead aim for improvement. Try to constantly improve by a tiny little bit every day. Get in the habit of asking yourself, "How could I do it a little better this time?" Keep climbing, keep discovering, and keep pushing your limits. That's where real satisfaction and progress are.

●●●

완벽을 좇으며 자신을 지치게 하지 마.

알다시피, 완벽은 신기루 같아. 멀리서 보면 진짜처럼 보이지만 가까이 다가갈수록 멀어지거든. 산을 오르다 정상에 도달했다고 생각했는데, 그 뒤에 또 다른 봉우리가 있는 걸 발견한 것처럼 말이야.

아름다움은 산을 오르는 그 자체, 새로운 경관을 발견하고, 도전을 이겨 내고, 매 걸음마다 더 단단해지는 과정에 있어. 그게 바로 향상이야. 완벽이라는 지점에 도달하는 게 아니라 매일 성장하고 발전하고 더 나아지는 거야.

그러니 완벽을 좇느라 스스로를 지치게 하지 말고, 대신 나아지는 것을 목표로 해. 매일 아주 조금씩 끊임없이 나아지려고 해 봐. 자신에게 '이번엔 어떻게 하면 조금 더 잘할 수 있을까?'라고 질문하는 습관을 들여 봐. 계속 오르고, 계속 발견하고, 계속 한계를 밀어내는 거야. 진정한 만족과 발전은 거기에 있어.

mirage 신기루 | **lie in** 놓여 있다 | **process** 발전, 진보

Let Go of Regrets.

Getting rid of regret is like clearing old clutter from your room. It frees up space for new, positive experiences. Holding onto regrets is like carrying a backpack full of stones; it only weighs you down. A good way to overcome regret is to turn it into a learning experience and resolve to change what you're doing, starting now.

A common regret people have is that they focus too much on work but not enough on family. Ask yourself, "Have I fallen into this trap?" If you have, then pull out your calendar immediately and schedule regular family time so that you can avoid suffering this regret in the future. You know that family is critically important, so be sure to make it a part of your regular schedule.

Whatever you do, though, don't dwell on the regret. Instead, work to ensure that you never experience this exact same regret again. Transforming regret into a lesson and action helps you grow and move forward. Regret no longer!

●●●

후회를 내려놓아.

후회를 없애는 건 방에서 오래된 잡동사니를 치우는 일과 같아. 새롭고 긍정적인 경험을 위해 공간을 만드는 거지. 후회를 붙잡고 있는 건 돌멩이로 가득 찬 배낭을 메고 다니는 거나 다름없어. 그저 너를 내리누를 뿐이지. 후회를 이겨 내는 좋은 방법은 그걸 배움의 경험으로 바꾸고, 해 오던 방식을 바꾸겠다고 결심한 다음, 바로 시작하는 거야.

사람들이 흔히 하는 후회는 일에 너무 집중하느라 가족을 소홀히 했다는 거야. '나도 이 함정에 빠졌나?' 자신에게 물어봐. 만약 그렇다면, 미래에 이런 후회로 고통받는 걸 피할 수 있도록, 당장 달력을 꺼내 규칙적으로 가족과 보내는 시간을 정하도록 해. 알다시피 가족은 정말 중요하니까 반드시 규칙적인 일정으로 만들도록 해.

무엇보다 중요한 건 후회를 곱씹지 않는 거야. 그 대신, 다시는 똑같은 후회를 반복하지 않도록 노력해. 후회를 교훈과 행동으로 바꾸면, 성장하고 앞으로 나아가는 데 도움이 돼. 더 이상 후회하지 마!

DATE ______ / ______ / ______

get rid of 없애다 | clutter 잡동사니 | overcome 이겨 내다, 극복하다 |
dwell on 곱씹다 | transform 바꾸다

This Is the One Life You've Got.

Life isn't meant to be lived huddled in a corner, no matter how safe it feels.

Life is a great adventure waiting to happen, filled with unexpected and exciting events. The safety of the corner may protect you, but it also limits you. It's outside in the unpredictability, where the miracles happen. It's where you find out what you're truly capable of, where you meet people who change your perspective, where you stumble and fall, but learn how to get back up stronger. Every day offers a new scene in your adventure, a chance to explore something unfamiliar, to learn, to grow, to laugh, and to love.

So, step out from that corner, face the unknown with a spark in your eyes, and live a life overflowing with adventure. It's the one life you've got, make it count!

•••

인생은 단 한 번뿐이야.

구석에 웅크리고 사는 게 아무리 안전하게 느껴져도, 삶은 그렇게 사는 걸 의미하지 않아.

삶은 뜻밖의 흥미로운 일들로 가득한, 아직 펼쳐지지 않은 위대한 모험이야. 구석이라는 안전장치가 너를 보호해 줄 수도 있지만, 널 제한하기도 해. 기적이 일어나는 곳은 예측할 수 없는 바깥세상이거든. 그곳은 진정한 능력을 발견하는 곳, 시각을 바꿔 줄 사람들을 만나는 곳, 비틀거리고 넘어지지만 다시 일어나 더 강해지는 법을 배우는 곳이야. 하루하루가 그 모험 속에 새로운 장면, 낯선 것을 탐험하고 배우고 성장하고 웃고 사랑할 기회를 줘.

그러니 구석에서 벗어나 눈에 생기를 띠고 미지의 세상을 마주하고 모험으로 넘쳐 나는 삶을 살아. 인생은 단 한 번뿐이니, 소중히 여겨!

huddle 웅크리다 | stumble 비틀거리다 |
spark 생기, 불꽃 | overflow with 넘쳐 나다

Phase

3

Launch Action Steps

행동 단계 시작하기

"It's not what happens to you in life that counts.
Rather, it's what you do about it that really matters."

-from Day 26-

"삶에서 무슨 일이 일어나는지는 중요하지 않아.
그보다 그 일에 대해 무얼 하느냐가 정말로 중요해."

Pen Gratitude to Exude Positivity.

How about we bring back a bit of old-school charm with thank-you notes? Once a week, let's take a moment to pen down a few lines to someone who's made a difference in our week. It could be a friend, a teacher, or hey, even the barista who nails your coffee every time. It doesn't have to be fancy, just a simple note or email to say, "Hey, I noticed what you did, and I'm really thankful for it." It's a small act, but it can mean a lot.

And you know what? It not only makes their day a bit brighter, but it feels pretty good for us too. It's like a little burst of positivity, and who knows, it might just cause others to show their gratitude, too. Try it!

•••

긍정이 배어 나오는 감사를 적어 봐.

감사 편지로 옛 감성을 조금 되살려 보면 어때? 일주일에 한 번, 우리의 한 주에 변화를 준 사람에게 글을 몇 줄 적는 시간을 가져 보는 거야. 친구나 선생님, 매번 커피를 완벽하게 만들어 주는 바리스타라도 좋아. 거창할 필요 없어. '당신이 뭘 해 줬는지 알고 있어요. 정말 고마워요'라고 말하는 간단한 메모나 이메일이면 돼. 작은 행동이지만 큰 의미가 될 수 있어.

그리고 그거 알아? 그걸로 그들의 하루가 조금 환해질 뿐 아니라 우리 기분도 꽤 좋아질 거야. 마치 긍정의 작은 폭발 같은 거라서, 다른 사람들이 감사를 표현하게 하는 계기가 될 수도 있어. 한번 해 봐!

old-school charm 구식의 매력 | barista 바리스타 |
nail 완벽하게 하다 | fancy 거창한, 엄청난 | burst 폭발

Even the Best Athletes Have Coaches.

You know that myth that says you should tackle everything alone? Well, that's just not true. Even the best athletes have coaches, right? They get that outside perspective to level up. Needing help isn't a sign you're lacking—it just means you're smart enough to get the right tools.

So, if something's bothering you, whether it's your thoughts, skills, or finances, why not seek out an expert? Find a therapist, a coach, or a financial pro. These folks are equipped to help you overcome obstacles and thrive. Bringing in an outside perspective? Sometimes that's the key. It's not about giving up; it's about teaming up to conquer whatever comes your way.

●●●

최고의 운동선수들도 코치가 있어.

모든 걸 혼자 감당해야 한다고 말하는 통념 있잖아? 음, 그거 사실이 아니야. 최고의 운동선수들도 코치를 두지? 실력을 키우려고 외부의 시각을 받아들이는 거야. 도움을 요청한다는 게 부족하다는 신호는 아니야. 꽤 현명하게 적절한 도구를 얻는다는 뜻일 뿐이지.

무언가가 거슬린다면, 그게 생각이든, 기술이든, 재정이든, 전문가를 찾아보는 건 어때? 심리 치료사, 코치, 재정 전문가를 찾아봐. 이 사람들은 네가 장애물을 극복하고 성장하게 도와줄 능력이 있어. 외부의 관점을 받아들이는 거? 때로는 그게 해결책이야. 포기하는 게 아니고, 앞길을 막는 게 뭐든, 이겨 내려고 협력하는 거야.

lacking 부족한 | finance 재정, 경제 |
therapist 심리 치료사 | thrive 성공하다

The Chance to Truly Master Vocab.

Let me share a little tip about learning English words. A lot of people learn just one meaning of a word and don't realize that most words have multiple meanings. This is why you've probably said, "I know the words, but I don't get the sentence." You probably don't truly understand one or more of those words.

So, when reading, if a sentence feels a bit weird even though you feel certain you know all the words, it's a cue to check the dictionary. Maybe there's a common usage of a word you're not aware of. Don't miss this chance to really learn! It's tempting to think you've got the meaning just from context, but that can be tricky, even for native speakers.

Always double-check words, even familiar ones, to be sure you're on the right track. It's a small step, but it makes a big difference!

●●●

진정으로 어휘를 익히는 기회

영어 단어를 익히는 작은 팁을 나눠 줄게. 많은 사람이 단어의 한 가지 뜻만 익히고, 대부분 단어에 여러 의미가 있다는 걸 간과해. 이게 바로 네가 '단어는 다 아는데 문장이 이해가 안 돼'라고 말해 왔던 이유일 거야. 아마도 그 단어 중 하나나 그 이상을 확실히 이해하지 못한 걸 거야.

그러니까 다 아는 단어라고 확신하는데도 문장을 읽을 때 조금 이상하게 느껴진다면, 그건 사전을 찾아보라는 신호야. 어쩌면 네가 알지 못했던 단어의 일반적인 용법이 있을 수도 있거든. 정말로 배울 기회를 놓치지 마! 문맥만 보고 그 의미를 안다고 믿고 싶겠지만, 사실 원어민에게조차 까다로운 문제일 수 있어.

그러니 익숙한 단어라도 꼭 올바르게 이해하도록, 항상 한 번 더 확인하도록 해. 작은 한 걸음이지만 커다란 차이를 만들 거야!

weird 이상한 | cue 신호 | context 문맥 | tricky 까다로운, 미묘한

20 Dreams Daily.

Let's talk about a little habit that could be a game changer. Every morning, sometime after you wake up, perhaps as you nibble on your breakfast, write down a list of 20 things you want to achieve. 20 things might sound like a lot, but don't sweat it. Just write down the first 20 things that pop into your head, big or small, such as invest in an index fund, take a trip to Bali Island, develop an app, master the art of coffee making, or start an online business. Avoid looking at what you've written on past days.

The idea of the exercise is to see what your subconscious mind thinks is important right now. This exercise will help direct your mind to the goals you truly want and give you the focus and energy to achieve the most important items on the list. Do this exercise every day for 30 days, and your life will never be the same.

●●●

매일의 스무 가지 꿈

삶을 바꿀 수 있는 작은 습관에 관해 이야기해 보자. 매일 아침에 일어나서, 아마도 아침을 조금씩 먹으면서, 이루고 싶은 스무 가지를 적어 봐. 스무 가지가 많게 느껴질 수도 있지만 걱정하지 마. 그냥 머리에 처음 떠오르는 스무 가지를 써 내려가면 돼. 예를 들어, 인덱스 펀드에 투자하기, 발리 여행하기, 앱 개발하기, 커피 내리는 기술 익히기, 온라인 사업 시작하기처럼 크든 작든 상관없어. 과거에 쓴 것은 보지 않도록 해.

이 연습의 목적은 무의식이 바로 지금 중요하다고 생각하는 게 뭔지 확인하는 거야. 이 연습은 진정으로 원하는 목표로 마음이 향하도록 도와주고, 목록에서 가장 중요한 항목들을 이루게 해 줄 집중력과 에너지를 줄 거야. 이 연습을 매일 30일 동안 해 봐. 삶이 완전히 달라질 거야.

nibble 조금씩 먹다 | **pop into** 떠오르다 |
invest 투자하다 | **index fund** 인덱스 펀드

Don't Set Unrealistic Standards.

It's a simple yet profound truth that no one is perfect. We all come with our strengths and areas we could improve. It's essential to remember this, especially when it comes to relationships. Expecting someone to be perfect sets an unrealistic standard, both for them and for yourself. It can lead to disappointment and unnecessary tension.

Instead, it's healthier to embrace and accept each other's imperfections. It's in these imperfect moments, the missteps, and the laughter that follows, where the real bonding happens. It's what makes a relationship genuine and enduring.

So, let's be kinder to each other, practice patience, and remember that in a world where no one is perfect, understanding and acceptance are what truly build a solid foundation.

●●●

비현실적인 기준을 세우지 마.

단순하지만 뿌리 깊은 진실은 누구도 완벽하지 않다는 거야. 우리는 모두 강점과 개선할 수 있는 부분이 있어. 이 사실을 기억하는 건, 특히 관계에 있어서 매우 중요해. 누군가가 완벽하기를 기대하는 건, 그 사람뿐 아니라 자신에게도 비현실적인 기준을 세우는 거야. 그런 기대는 실망과 불필요한 긴장으로 이어질 수 있어.

대신, 더 건강한 방식은 서로의 불완전함을 감싸안고 받아들이는 거야. 이 불완전한 순간, 실수, 그 뒤에 따라오는 웃음에서 진짜 유대가 생겨. 그런 유대가 관계를 진실하고 오래가게 해.

그러니 서로에게 좀 더 친절해지고, 인내하며, 누구도 완벽하지 않은 세상에서 이해와 수용이야말로 정말 단단한 기반을 쌓는 것임을 기억하자.

profound 뿌리 깊은 | tension 긴장 | misstep 실수 |
bond 유대 | enduring 지속하는

It's Not What Happens…

Life is a mixed bag, with lots of ups and downs. Yet, it's not really about the situations you find yourself in, but rather how you react to them.

When life gives you a lemon, you have two choices: to let it defeat you or to make lemonade. Each challenge is a chance to learn and grow, to become stronger and wiser. It's your actions in the face of adversity that say who you truly are. So, no matter what comes your way, choose to face it directly, learn from it, and use it as a stepping stone towards becoming a better version of yourself.

Remember! It's not what happens to you in life that counts. Rather, it's what you do about it that really matters.

●●●

일어난 일이 중요한 게 아니라…

인생은 기복이 아주 많은, 뒤섞인 자루야. 하지만 정말 중요한 건 네가 처한 상황이 아니라, 네 반응이야.

삶이 레몬(어려움, 시련—역주)을 건넬 때 선택지는 두 가지야. 좌절하거나 그걸로 레모네이드를 만드는 거지. 어려움 하나하나가 배우고 성장하고, 더 강해지고 현명해질 기회야. 역경을 마주할 때 하는 행동이 네가 진정으로 어떤 사람인지 말해 줘. 그러니 어떤 일이 닥쳐도 그걸 똑바로 마주하고, 거기서 배우고, 더 나은 자신이 되는 발판으로 활용하도록 해.

기억해! 삶에서 무슨 일이 일어나는지는 중요하지 않아. 그보다 그 일에 대해 무얼 하느냐가 정말로 중요해.

defeat 좌절시키다 | wiser 더 현명한 |
directly 똑바로 | stepping stone 발판, 디딤돌

Experience True Happiness.

One of the best ways to feel truly happy is by giving back and helping others. When you lend a hand, not only do you make someone else's day a little brighter, but you also get this warm and fuzzy feeling inside. It's like a happiness boost for both you and the person you've helped.

So, look for ways you can volunteer in your community or simply help out a friend or even a stranger. It doesn't have to be anything big or take much time out of your day. Sometimes, even the smallest act of kindness can make a big difference. When you start to see the smiles on people's faces, you'll understand just how powerful giving back can be. Do something for someone else right now and see how you feel.

●●●

진정한 행복을 경험하도록 해.

진정으로 행복을 느끼는 가장 좋은 방법 하나는 나눔을 실천하고 다른 사람들을 돕는 거야. 도움을 주면, 누군가의 하루가 조금 더 환해질 뿐 아니라 네 마음에도 따뜻하고 포근한 느낌이 생겨. 너와 네가 도와준 사람, 둘 다에게 행복 충전 같은 거지.

그러니 공동체에서 자원봉사 할 수 있는 방법을 찾아보거나 단순히 친구나 모르는 사람에게라도 도움을 줘. 거창하거나 시간이 오래 걸리는 일이 아니어도 돼. 때로는 아주 작은 친절도 커다란 차이를 만들 수 있어.

사람들의 얼굴에 미소가 떠오를 때 나눔이 얼마나 강력한지 알게 될 거야. 지금 당장 누군가를 위해 무언가를 하고 어떤 기분인지 확인해 봐.

give back 돌려주다, 나누다 | warm and fuzzy 따뜻하고 포근한 |
volunteer 자원봉사를 하다 | community 공동체

Unsuccessful Effort Is Another Form of Success.

You know what's cool? Every time you put in some effort, it's like adding a tiny, yet powerful, piece to your life's puzzle. Yeah, sometimes things don't go the way you planned, and it feels like you've been surrounded by obstacles. But guess what? It's not a dead end, it's an avenue to achievement. Even if things don't go well, each effort gives you wisdom.

You learn a little something, change the placement of your puzzle pieces, and bam! You're one step closer to getting it next time. It's all about gathering these bits of knowledge from every effort, even the ones that seem to go badly. Also, just because you won't be able to finish the puzzle in one go, don't let that deter you from jumping in or changing your approach. Remember that each effort, successful or not, is still meaningful.

If it doesn't work, congrats! You have successfully crossed another method off your list of things to try, which means you're one step closer to hanging that puzzle on the wall. Keep going!

●●●

성공하지 못한 노력도 성공의 또 다른 모습이야.

근사한 거 알려 줄까? 매번 노력을 쏟을 때, 그건 마치 삶의 퍼즐에 작지만 강력한 조각 하나를 더하는 것과 같아. 그래, 때로는 상황이 계획대로 흘러가지 않아 장애물에 둘러싸여 있는 듯 느껴지기도 해. 하지만 그거 알아? 그게 막다른 길이 아니라 성취로 가는 길이란 걸.

일이 잘 풀리지 않더라도, 모든 노력은 지혜를 줘. 작은 무언가를 배우고 퍼즐 조각들의 위치를 바꾸고 나면, 짜잔! 다음번엔 성공에 한 걸음 더 가까워져. 중요한 건 모든 노력에서, 겉보기에 실패한 듯 보이는 노력에서도, 이런 작은 지식을 얻는 거야. 그리고 한 번에 퍼즐을 끝낼 수 없다고 해서, 시작하거나 접근 방식을 바꾸는 걸 주저하지 마. 노력은, 성공하든 하지 못하든 여전히 의미가 있다는 걸 기억해.

잘 안됐다면, 축하해! 시도해 볼 것 목록에서 성공적으로 한 가지 방법을 지워 냈으니, 벽에 퍼즐을 거는 데 한 걸음 더 가까워졌다는 의미야. 계속 나아가!

tiny 작은 | **puzzle** 퍼즐 | **surround** 둘러싸다 | **gather** 얻다, 모으다

Stop Blaming Yourself.

You know, blaming yourself and feeling guilty doesn't help at all. It just makes you feel down and zaps your energy. Letting go of self-blame is like breaking free from invisible chains. Remember, making mistakes is just a part of learning and growing, not a reason to be tough on yourself.

Whenever you think, "I messed up," try to pause and ask yourself, "What can I learn from this?" Say you didn't do great in a presentation. Instead of sinking into self-blame, think about how to do better next time or get some feedback. Often, things need more practice than we first think, and that's perfectly okay. What you want to do is turn a tough moment into a chance to grow.

Everyone has days when things don't go right, but what matters is how you learn and bounce back from them. Keep growing!

●●●

자신을 탓하지 마.

자신을 탓하고 죄책감을 느끼는 건 전혀 도움이 되지 않아. 그저 우울해지고 기운 빠질 뿐이야. 자기 비난을 내려놓는 건 보이지 않는 사슬에서 벗어나는 것과 같아. 실수하는 건 그저 배움과 성장의 일부분이지, 자신에게 엄격하게 대할 이유가 아니란 걸 기억하도록 해.

'망쳐 버렸어'라는 생각이 들 때마다 잠시 멈춰 자신에게 '여기서 배울 수 있는 게 뭐지?'라고 물어봐. 발표를 잘하지 못했다고 해 보자. 자기 비난에 빠지는 대신 다음엔 더 잘할 방법이나 피드백을 받을 방법을 생각해 봐. 많은 경우, 처음 생각했던 것보다 더 많은 연습이 필요하겠지만, 그건 정말 괜찮아. 해야 할 일은 힘든 순간을 성장하는 기회로 바꾸는 거야.

누구에게나 일이 잘 풀리지 않는 날이 있지만, 중요한 건 거기서 무엇을 배우고 어떻게 다시 일어서는가야. 계속 성장해 나가!

zap 없애다, 해치우다 | invisible 보이지 않는 |
mess up 망치다 | sink 빠지다, 가라앉다

The View Is Much Better from the Top.

It's tempting to wish that life were easier, or that things were cheaper, but that's like hoping a mountain changes its height so it's easier to climb. It's a passive approach. However, aspiring to be better and have more is like training yourself to climb higher peaks, or saving up for what you desire. It's taking an active approach that gives you the power to improve your life.

Life's going to throw challenges either way, but by planning to be better, you're essentially gearing up to meet those challenges head-on. So, whenever you find yourself wishing for things to be easier or cheaper, catch yourself. Turn that wish towards personal growth and increased earning instead.

Trust me, the view is much better from the top, and the sense of accomplishment when you can afford what you want is awesome.

●●●

풍경은 정상에서 보는 게 훨씬 더 멋져.

인생이 좀 더 쉬웠다면, 모든 게 좀 더 저렴했다면, 하고 바라겠지만, 그건 마치 산이 오르기 쉽게 그 높이를 낮춰 주길 바라는 것과 같아. 이는 수동적인 접근 방식이야. 하지만 더 나아지고 더 많이 갖고 싶은 열망은 더 높은 봉우리에 오르도록 훈련하거나 원하는 물건을 사기 위해 저축하는 것과 마찬가지야. 이는 삶을 향상할 힘을 주는 능동적인 접근 방식을 취하는 거야.

삶은 어느 쪽을 택하든 시련을 주겠지만, 더 나아지도록 계획하면, 본질적으로 그 시련을 정면으로 맞설 준비를 갖추게 돼. 그러니 무언가가 더 쉽거나 저렴하길 바라는 순간, 거기서 멈춰. 대신, 그 바람을 개인적 성장과 인상된 소득으로 바꿔 봐.

날 믿어, 풍경은 정상에서 보는 게 훨씬 더 멋지고, 원하는 걸 가질 여유가 생길 때 그 성취감은 굉장해.

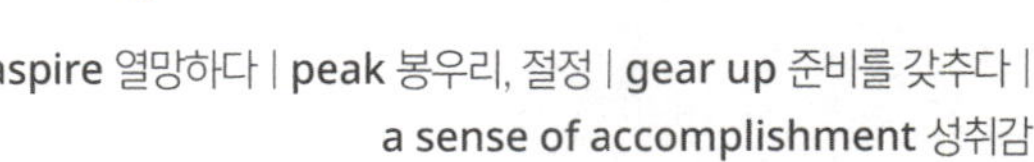

aspire 열망하다 | peak 봉우리, 절정 | gear up 준비를 갖추다 |
a sense of accomplishment 성취감

Phase

Gradually Advance

서서히 나아가기

"With every step taken with grit,
doubt falls further behind,
and your dreams come closer."
-from Day 36-

"근성을 가지고 한 걸음 한 걸음 내디딜 때마다
의심은 더 멀어지고 꿈은 더 가까워져."

The Currency of Gratitude Is Unlimited.

Gratitude is indeed a special kind of currency, one that doesn't disappear no matter how much you spend. It's a perspective that allows you to see the value in what you have, the people around you, and even the seemingly small moments in life.

The beautiful thing is, the more you spend this currency by expressing your thankfulness, the richer you become in happiness and contentment. It's like an investment that only grows over time, never losing its value. And the cool part? There's no limit to how much of this currency you can make.

Every moment presents an opportunity to appreciate and feel grateful for the good things in your life. It's a habit that not only improves your own life but also makes the world around you a bit brighter.

●●●

감사라는 화폐는 무제한이야.

감사는 정말 특별한 종류의 화폐로, 아무리 많이 써도 사라지지 않아. 감사는 네가 가지고 있는 가치에서, 주변 사람들에게서, 겉보기에는 작은 삶의 순간에서도 가치를 보는 시각이야.

놀라운 건, 이 화폐를 고마움을 표현하는 데 쓰면 쓸수록 행복과 만족이 더 커진다는 점이야. 시간이 지나야만 자라나는, 절대 가치를 잃지 않는 투자나 다름없어. 그리고 근사한 점은? 이 화폐를 만들 수 있는 양에는 제한이 없다는 거야.

매 순간이 삶의 좋은 일들을 알아보고 감사할 기회를 줘. 감사는 자신의 삶을 더 나아지게 할 뿐 아니라 주변 세상을 좀 더 환하게 비춰 주는 습관이야.

currency 화폐 | disappear 사라지다 |
perspective 시각, 관점 | brighter 더 밝은

Take It Step by Step.

Feeling overwhelmed? I get it. When you're facing something huge, it's like staring at a mountain and thinking, "How am I gonna climb that?" But here's the thing: Don't look at the whole mountain—just focus on the next few steps.

Break that big, scary problem into smaller, manageable pieces. Then, start knocking them out, one by one. Each step you take? That's a win! And it adds up. Before you know it, you'll look back and see how far you've come.

So, remember, you don't have to solve everything at once. Take it step by step, and you'll get there in the end. Cool, isn't it?

한 걸음씩 나아가.

버겁게 느껴져? 이해해. 엄청난 무언가를 마주하고 있을 때, 그건 마치 산을 응시하며 '저걸 어떻게 오르지?' 하고 생각하는 것과 같아. 하지만 그럴 땐 산 전체를 보지 마. 그냥 다음 몇 걸음에 집중해.

크고 무서운 문제를 더 작고 다루기 쉬운 조각으로 쪼개는 거야. 그다음, 그 조각들을 하나씩 쓰러뜨려. 한 걸음씩 나아가는 거? 그게 이기는 거야! 그리고 그건 쌓여. 알아차리기도 전에, 뒤돌아보면 네가 얼마나 멀리 와 있는지 알게 될 거야.

그러니 기억해, 한 번에 모든 걸 해결하지 않아도 돼. 한 걸음씩 나아가다 보면 결국 그곳에 닿을 거야. 근사하지 않아?

overwhelmed 어쩔 줄 모르는 | stare 응시하다, 빤히 보다 |
scary 무서운 | knock out 쓰러뜨리다

Seek Multiple Benefits.

Whatever you're doing, always aim to "kill at least two birds with one stone." Constantly seeking and taking shortcuts often leads to wasted time without gaining anything of value.

Take test-taking, for instance. If you genuinely focus on improving your abilities, you won't just pass the test; you'll also function better in your field afterward. It's like when you exercise, you're not just building muscle, you're also improving your overall health. So, always look for ways to maximize the benefits of your efforts. This approach not only saves you time but also ensures that you get the most out of your hard work.

Remember, it's not just about working hard; it's about working smart.

●●●

여러 가지 이익을 찾아봐.

무엇을 하고 있든, 항상 '돌 하나로 적어도 새 두 마리를 잡는' 걸 목표로 해. 끊임없이 지름길을 찾고 그 지름길로 가다 보면, 시간만 낭비하고 아무런 가치도 얻지 못하는 경우가 종종 있어.

시험을 예로 들어 보자. 진심으로 능력을 키우는 데 집중한다면, 시험을 통과할 뿐 아니라 이후 그 분야에서도 더 잘 해낼 거야. 운동할 때도 마찬가지로, 근육만 만드는 데 그치지 않고 전반적인 건강도 나아질 거야. 그러니 항상 노력에 따른 이익을 극대화할 방법을 찾도록 해. 이런 접근법은 시간을 절약할 뿐 아니라, 네 노력에서 최대한을 끌어내게 해.

기억해, 중요한 건 열심히 하는 것만이 아니라, 현명하게 하는 거야.

constantly 끊임없이 | genuinely 진심으로 |
maximize 최대화하다 | ensure 보증하다

Don't Just Focus on "What's in It for Me?"

Listen, when it comes to goals, it's not just about the end game—the thing you want to have or the place you want to get to. Nah, it's way deeper than that.

The true value is who you become while you're reaching for that goal. I mean, sure, scoring that college acceptance or getting that job is awesome. But the person you evolve into? That's the real prize. You learn, you struggle, you adapt, and all that shapes you into someone better.

So, don't just focus on the "what will I get" part. Shift that thinking, and ask yourself, "What will I become?" Because, trust me, the growth along the way? That's what you'll carry with you, long after you've achieved that goal.

•••

'나에게 무슨 이익이 있을까?'에만 집중하지 마.

자, 목표에 대해 말하자면, 중요한 건 최종 결과(갖고 싶은 물건이나 가고 싶은 장소)가 아니야. 아니, 그보다 훨씬 더 깊은 거야.

그 진정한 가치는 그 목표에 다가가는 동안 네가 어떤 사람이 되는지에 있어. 내 말은, 물론 대학에 입학하거나 직장에 취업하는 건 굉장해. 하지만 발전한 너라는 사람은? 그게 진짜 보상이야. 배우고, 부딪히고, 적응하고, 그 모든 과정이 너를 더 나은 사람으로 만들어 줘.

그러니 '무엇을 얻을까'에만 집중하지 마. 생각을 바꿔서 '어떤 사람이 될까?'를 물어. 왜냐하면, 그 과정에서의 성장? 그게 바로 목표를 이룬 뒤에도 오랫동안, 너와 함께할 것이니까.

DATE _____ / _____ / _____

way 훨씬 | score 점수를 받다 |
evolve 발전시키다, 진화하다 | struggle 싸우다, 발버둥치다

Before You Get Angry...

It's quite easy to jump to conclusions when your other half says or does something that irks you. However, it's essential to pause and make sure that you've understood their intentions correctly. Misunderstandings are a common part of relationships, and they can lead to unnecessary anger if not clarified.

Before you say something you'll regret, take a moment to ask them about their true intentions. More often than not, you'll find that they meant something entirely different from what you initially thought. When they clarify themselves, believe them. It's a simple yet powerful way to maintain harmony and mutual respect in relationships.

This habit promotes open communication and prevents minor issues from becoming significant issues.

●●●

화내기 전에...

배우자가 짜증 나는 말이나 행동을 할 때, 성급하게 결론 내리기는 정말 쉬워. 하지만 잠시 멈춰 그들의 의도를 제대로 이해했는지 확인하는 건 꼭 필요해. 오해는 관계에서 흔한 부분이고, 명확히 하지 않으면 불필요한 화를 불러일으킬 수 있거든.

후회할 말을 하기 전에, 그들의 진짜 의도를 물어보는 시간을 가져. 대개는 처음 생각한 것과는 전혀 다른 의미였다는 걸 알게 될 거야. 그들이 분명하게 말해 주면 그 말을 믿어. 그게 관계에서 조화와 상호 존중을 유지하는 단순하지만 강력한 방법이야.

이런 습관은 열린 대화를 촉진하고 사소한 갈등이 커다란 문제가 되는 걸 막아 줘.

irk 짜증 나게 하다 | intention 의도 | clarify 분명히 말하다 |
promote 촉진하다 | minor 사소한

Leave Doubt Behind You.

Picture life as a long marathon filled with the highs of achievement and the lows of uncertainties. Now, imagine your dreams as the finish line you're working to reach. The pace you run this marathon is not about speed, but endurance, and that enduring pace is fueled by grit.

Grit keeps your legs moving when doubt tries to slow you down. With every step taken with grit, doubt falls further behind, and your dreams come closer. It's about outrunning the whisper of doubt with the loud echo of grit, every step of the way. So, put on your shoes, set a pace filled with determination, and run towards your dreams, leaving doubt behind.

●●●

의심을 버려.

삶을 최고의 성취와 최하의 불확실성으로 채워진 긴 마라톤으로 상상해 봐. 그리고 꿈은 도달하려고 애쓰는 결승선으로 떠올려 봐. 이 마라톤을 뛰는 속도에서 중요한 건 속력이 아니라 지구력이야. 그리고 그 지구력 있는 속도는 근성에서 연료를 얻어.

의심이 너를 느리게 하려 할 때, 근성은 계속 다리를 움직이게 해. 근성을 가지고 한 걸음 한 걸음 내디딜 때마다 의심은 더 멀어지고 꿈은 더 가까워져. 모든 걸음마다 의심의 속삭임을 근성이라는 커다란 메아리로 앞지르는 게 중요해.

그러니 신발 끈을 꽉 매고 결의를 가득 채워 속도를 정하고, 의심을 버리고 꿈을 향해 달려.

pace 속도, 보폭 | endurance 지구력, 인내 | fuel by ~로 연료를 공급하다 |
whisper 속삭임 | determination 결의, 결심

Train Your Mind to Focus on the Present.

You've probably heard people talk about the benefits of mindfulness meditation before. It's such a good habit to get into. By practicing mindfulness, you can train your mind to focus on the present moment, which can significantly reduce stress and boost your overall happiness.

You don't have to sit there for hours, either. Simply taking a few minutes each day to focus on your breath or practicing some deep breathing exercises can make a huge difference. Even just taking a few moments to pause, breathe, and be present can be an incredibly powerful tool in creating a happier, more peaceful life.

Right now, close your eyes and take 5 slow breaths, counting like this: breathe in for 4, hold for 4, breathe out for 4, hold for 4. Repeat 5 times. See? You feel better already, don't you?

●●●

현재에 집중하도록 마음을 훈련하도록 해.

사람들이 마음 챙김 명상의 장점에 관해 이야기하는 걸 들어본 적 있을 거야. 그건 정말 좋은 습관이지. 마음 챙김을 실천하면, 마음이 지금 이 순간에 집중하도록 훈련할 수 있고, 그렇게 하면 스트레스를 크게 줄이고 전반전인 행복감을 끌어 올릴 수 있어.

몇 시간이나 앉아 있을 필요도 없어. 단순히 하루에 몇 분을 할애해서 호흡에 집중하거나 심호흡을 연습하는 것만으로도 큰 차이를 만들 수 있거든. 단 몇 분이라도 잠시 멈춰 호흡하고 현재에 머무르는 건 더 행복하고 평화로운 삶을 만드는 엄청나게 강력한 도구가 될 수 있어.

지금 당장 눈을 감고 느리게 다섯 번 호흡하며 이렇게 수를 세어 봐. 넷을 세며 숨을 들이쉬고, 넷을 세며 숨을 멈추고, 넷을 세며 숨을 내쉬고, 넷을 세며 숨을 멈춰. 이렇게 다섯 번 반복하는 거야. 어때? 벌써 기분이 나아지지 않았어?

mindfulness meditation 마음 챙김 명상 | **train** 훈련하다 |
reduce 줄이다 | **boost** 끌어 올리다

Green & Growing or Brown & Dying.

Hey, you know what they say, right? Life's always in motion. You're either getting better, or you're falling behind. Think of yourself as a plant—either green and growing or brown and withering.

Trust me, nothing in life stays the same; it's like a river, always flowing. So, make sure you're swimming in the right direction! Whether it's your grades, your friendships, or even your personal goals, always aim to improve. Even the small steps count, you know. Just don't get too comfy and think you've got it all figured out because there's always room to grow.

So, let's focus on the here and now, make those wise choices, and keep on climbing. You're capable of so much; don't let yourself forget it.

•••

푸르게 자라나느냐, 갈색으로 시들어 가느냐.

이런 말, 알지? 삶은 늘 움직여. 나아지고 있거나 뒤처지고 있거나, 둘 중 하나야. 자신을 식물이라고 생각해 봐. 푸르게 자라나거나 갈색으로 시들어 가거나야.

날 믿어, 삶에서 변하지 않는 건 없어. 강처럼 항상 흐르지. 그러니 옳은 방향으로 헤엄치고 있는지 확인해! 성적이든, 우정이든, 개인적 목표든, 항상 나아지는 걸 목표로 해. 작은 발걸음도 의미가 있어. 너무 편안해지지도, 다 안다고 생각하지도 마. 성장할 여지는 얼마든지 있으니까.

그러니 지금, 여기에 집중하고 현명한 선택을 하며 계속 올라가는 거야. 넌 역량이 아주 많아. 그걸 잊지 마.

motion 움직임 | wither 시들다 | flow 흐르다 | comfy 편한

Tailor Your Life.

Knowing yourself is about figuring out your unique traits. Honestly observing your actions (or asking someone who's close to tell you) is the key to doing so.

Take sleep, as an example. Some people are full of energy with just a few hours of sleep, while others need a solid 8 or 9 hours to feel their best. When it comes to learning, everyone's different too. You might be a visual learner who needs to see things, an auditory learner who needs to hear things, or maybe you're tactile and learn only by doing. And hey, some people are go-getters, always self-motivated, while others don't get off the sofa unless they get a push from others. If you do need a push, be sure to find someone who will push you.

By understanding who you are, you can tailor your life, learning, and work to suit you best. It also means not being too hard on yourself. So, discovering your true self is the secret weapon that can help you improve your quality of life, learning effectiveness, or work efficiency!

●●●

삶을 다듬어 봐.

자신을 안다는 건 자신만의 고유한 특성을 알아내는 거야. 자기 행동을 솔직하게 들여다보는 게 (혹은 가까운 사람에게 물어보는 게) 그렇게 하는 가장 좋은 방법이야.

수면을 예로 들어보자. 어떤 사람은 몇 시간만 자도 활기가 넘치지만, 어떤 사람은 8~9시간은 쭉 자야 최상의 컨디션을 느껴. 학습 방법도 모두 달라. 너는 눈으로 봐야 하는 시각형 학습자거나 귀로 들어야 하는 청각형 학습자, 아니면 직접 해 봐야 배우는 촉각형 학습자일 수도 있어. 그리고 어떤 사람은 항상 스스로 동기를 부여하는 행동파지만, 어떤 사람은 누군가가 등을 떠밀어 주지 않는 한 소파에서 일어나지 않아. 누군가의 밀어줌이 필요하다면 너를 밀어줄 사람을 찾아.

자신이 누구인지 이해하게 되면, 삶도, 배움도, 일도 자신에게 가장 잘 맞게 다듬을 수 있어. 그리고 그건 스스로에게 너무 엄격하지 않아도 된다는 의미기도 해. 그래서 진정한 자신을 발견해 나가는 일은 삶의 질이나 배움의 효과, 일의 효율이 올라가도록 돕는 비밀 무기야!

tailor 조정하다, 맞추다 | visual 시각의 |
auditory 청각의 | tactile 촉각의

Take the Road Less Traveled.

"Success is doing the opposite of what everybody else is doing." It's quite an interesting notion, isn't it? The idea that taking a different path could lead to success. It's like taking a less crowded street and discovering a shortcut.

The world is full of "accepted wisdoms" that often go unchallenged, mostly because they've been around for ages. But here's where it gets exciting—when you pause and question the usual way of doing things, you're already on a path less traveled. You start to see things from a fresh angle, which is often the starting point of innovation.

It's not about opposing the common just to be contrary, but about evaluating things with your own lens, gathering your own evidence. So, whenever you hear a "that's how it's always been done," question it instead of blindly following it.

•••

남들이 덜 다닌 길을 택해.

'성공은 모두가 하는 것과 반대로 하는 거야.' 꽤 흥미로운 생각이지, 안 그래? 남들과 다른 길을 택하는 건 성공으로 이어질 수 있다는 발상 말이야. 그건 마치 덜 붐비는 길을 가다가 지름길을 발견하는 것과도 같아.

세상은, 오랫동안 존재해 왔기 때문에 대개 문제 삼지 않는 '통념'으로 가득 해. 하지만 여기가 재미있는 부분이야. 잠시 멈춰서 늘 하던 방식에 의문을 품는 순간, 너는 이미 남들이 덜 다닌 길 위에 있는 거야. 새로운 시각으로 세상을 보게 되기 시작하고, 그건 종종 혁신의 출발점이 돼.

중요한 건 통념에 반대하는 것 자체가 아니라, 자신만의 시각으로 세상을 평가하고 자신만의 증거를 수집하는 거야. 그러니 '그게 늘 해 오던 방식이야'라는 말을 들을 때마다 맹목적으로 따르는 대신 질문을 던져.

notion 개념, 생각 | crowded 붐비는 | contrary 반대되는 |
evaluate 평가하다 | gather 수집하다

5

Persistently Execute

끈질기게 실행하기

"When the going gets tough, and you're ready
to throw in the towel, that's exactly when you should
challenge yourself to do just one more."
-from Day 46-

"상황이 힘들어져서 포기하려 할 때,
바로 그때가 한 번만 더 해 보라며
자신에게 도전해야 할 순간이야."

Share Gratitude at the Dining Table.

How about making mealtime more than just about food? While everyone's munching, let's get into the habit of sharing one thing we're each grateful for. It doesn't have to be big—maybe you aced a quiz, or you just enjoyed a workout at the gym. This isn't just about saying thanks, it's about feeling that warmth spread around the table.

It's pretty cool how sharing a simple piece of your day can make the food taste better and the bonds stronger. Plus, hearing what others appreciate can open your eyes to little blessings you might not have noticed. It's like a daily dose of feel-good right in the middle of the hustle and bustle.

Let's give it a go and see how our meals and our days get a whole lot richer.

●●●

저녁 식탁에서 감사를 나눠.

식사 시간을 단순히 음식을 먹는 시간 이상으로 만들어 보는 건 어때? 모두가 우적우적 먹는 동안, 각자 감사한 일 하나를 나누는 습관을 들여 보는 거야. 거창할 필요는 없어. 쪽지 시험을 잘 봤다거나 헬스장에서 즐겁게 운동한 것도 좋아. 중요한 건 단순히 고맙다고 말하는 게 아니라, 식탁 주변으로 퍼지는 따뜻함을 느끼는 거야.

꽤 근사한 건 하루의 단순한 조각을 나누는 것만으로도 음식은 더 맛있어지고 유대감은 더 깊어진다는 거야. 게다가 다른 이들이 무엇에 감사하는지 듣다 보면, 미처 알아차리지 못했던 작은 축복에 눈을 뜨게 돼. 그건 마치 분주한 하루의 한가운데서 하루치 기분 좋음을 복용하는 것과 같아.

한번 시도해 보고, 우리 식사와 하루가 얼마나 더 풍요로워지는지 확인해 보자.

munch 우적우적 먹다 | ace 이기다 | blessing 축복 |
dose 복용량 | hustle and bustle 북적북적, 분주함

Write Down Your Thoughts to Untangle Your Mind.

Ever feel like your thoughts are just swimming around in your head? We all get that way sometimes. One really good way to sort things out is to grab a notebook and start jotting down whatever's on your mind—your feelings, your worries, whatever it is. It's like you're decluttering a super messy room.

Once you've got all those thoughts out of your head and down on paper, they're not all jumbled up in your mind anymore. You can actually see them right in front of you. You might even start to see patterns or figure out what your next steps should be.

So, why not give it a try? Just let the words flow. It's a really useful way to help you navigate through the tough times.

●●●

생각을 글로 적어 엉킨 마음을 풀어 봐.

머릿속에서 생각이 그냥 이리저리 헤엄쳐 다니는 듯 느낀 적 있지? 우리 모두 이따금 그럴 때가 있어. 그걸 해결하는 정말 좋은 방법 하나는 공책을 꺼내 마음속에 있는 걸, 감정이든, 걱정이든, 뭐든 간에 써 보는 거야. 아주 어질러진 방을 치우는 것처럼 말이야.

머릿속에 있는 생각을 모두 꺼내 종이에 적고 나면, 그 생각은 더 이상 마음속에 얽혀 있지 않아. 바로 눈앞에서 실제로 볼 수 있어. 심지어 패턴이 보이거나 다음에 뭘 해야 할지 알게 될 수도 있어.

그러니 한번 해 보는 게 어때? 그냥 단어들이 흘러나오게 둬. 힘든 시기를 헤쳐 나가는 걸 도와줄 정말 유용한 방법이야.

sort out 해결하다 | **declutter** 치우다 |
jumbled 얽힌, 뒤죽박죽인 | **navigate** 헤쳐 나가다, 길을 찾다

Don't Wait Until "Ready"!

No matter how good your English vocabulary, grammar, pronunciation, or writing is, you might feel like it's not good enough to use. Of course, you can always learn new words and deepen your understanding of the words you already know. But remember, don't let the fear of not being "good enough" or not being "ready" hold you back. If you do, you might find yourself stuck in a loop of inaction.

The truth is you learn by doing. Every mistake is a lesson that brings you one step closer to fluency. So, go ahead, use what you know, and don't be afraid to make mistakes. Embrace the learning process and watch as your English skills blossom. You've got this!

● ● ●

'준비'될 때까지 기다리지 마!

영어 어휘나 문법, 발음, 쓰기 실력이 아무리 좋아도, 막상 써 보기엔 부족한 듯 느껴질지도 몰라. 물론 언제든 새로운 단어를 배우고, 이미 아는 단어를 더 깊이 이해할 수도 있어. 하지만 기억해, '충분'하지 않다거나 '준비'되지 않았다는 두려움에 발목 잡히지는 마. 그렇게 두면 고리 안에 갇혀 꼼짝 못 하는 자신을 발견하게 될 수도 있어.

사실, 우리는 직접 해 보면서 배워. 그리고 모든 실수는 유창함에 한 걸음 다가가는 교훈이야. 그러니 그냥 해 봐, 아는 걸 활용하고 실수하는 걸 두려워하지 마. 배우는 과정을 받아들이고 영어 실력이 꽃피우는 모습을 지켜보는 거야. 넌 할 수 있어!

stuck 갇힌 | loop 고리 | inaction 활동 부족 | blossom 꽃을 피우다

Remain Open and Welcome Change.

Listen, when you're starting any new adventure, it's super important to know what you want, alright? Think of it like this: you're going on a road trip—you know the end point, but you can get there in many different ways, each leading to a different adventure. So, don't be inflexible and stick to the first path you planned on taking.

Our world's packed with so many options that can be just as awesome as your end goal. Keep your mind open, be willing to accept changes, and soak up the experience. You'll see, sometimes these unplanned routes end up being the best part of the whole journey. You still reach your destination, but the whole ride was way more interesting and rewarding, wasn't it?

● ● ●

마음을 열고 변화를 받아들여.

들어 봐, 새로운 모험을 시작할 때, 자신이 원하는 게 뭔지 아는 건 굉장히 중요해, 알겠지? 이렇게 생각해 봐. 자동차 여행을 떠날 거야. 목적지는 알지만, 거기로 갈 수 있는 길은 아주 많고, 각각의 길은 다른 모험으로 이어져. 그러니 융통성 없이 굴지 말고, 처음 계획한 길만 고집하진 마.

세상은 마지막 목적지만큼이나 멋진, 수많은 선택지로 가득 차 있어. 마음을 열고, 기꺼이 변화를 받아들이고, 그 경험에 흠뻑 젖어 봐. 때로는 이런 계획에 없던 길이 전체 여정에서 최고의 순간이 되기도 해. 여전히 같은 목적지에 도착하지만, 전체 여정은 훨씬 더 흥미롭고 뿌듯했을 거야, 안 그래?

adventure 모험 | inflexible 융통성 없는 | packed 꽉 찬 |
option 선택지 | soak up 젖다, 잠기다

Jealousy and Control Are Like Relationship Poison.

If you're aiming for a rock-solid relationship, you've gotta build it on trust. That doesn't just mean not cheating, by the way. It's about being each other's rock: the person who's there no matter what life throws at you. Be consistent, don't make promises you can't keep, and whatever you do, be honest—even when it's hard.

But trust isn't just about being trusted; it's also about trusting them. Let them have their own space and friendships, and don't stress out over the small stuff. Jealousy and control are like relationship poison. And hey, mistakes happen, so forgiveness is key.

When you've got that trust, you've got a love that can withstand just about anything. Keep that in mind!

•••

질투와 통제는 관계를 병들게 하는 독약과 같아.

바위처럼 단단한 관계를 목표로 삼았다면, 관계를 신뢰 위에 쌓아야 해. 그렇지만, 그게 그저 속이지 않는 걸 의미하진 않아. 그건 서로에게 든든한 버팀목이 되어 주는 거야. 삶이 무엇을 내던지든 곁에 있어 주는 사람 말이야. 늘 한결같고, 지킬 수 없는 약속은 하지 말고, 무슨 일을 하든 정직해야 해. 힘들 때라도 그렇게 해야 해.

하지만 신뢰는 그저 신뢰받는 것만이 아니라 신뢰하는 것이기도 해. 그들이 자기만의 공간과 우정을 가지도록 놓아주고, 사소한 일에 스트레스받지 마. 질투와 통제는 관계를 병들게 하는 독약과 같아. 그리고 말이야, 실수는 누구나 하니까, 용서하는 게 중요해.

그런 신뢰가 쌓였을 때야 비로소 어떤 일에도 견딜 수 있는 사랑을 갖게 된 거야. 그걸 꼭 기억해!

음원 바로 듣기

Just One More.

When the going gets tough, and you're ready to throw in the towel, that's exactly when you should challenge yourself to do just one more. It could be anything—one more lap around the track, one more math problem, or one more run-through of your presentation. It's about pushing past that initial "I can't" and finding out that you actually can.

This isn't about overdoing it but about proving to yourself that you've got more in you than you thought. You'll be surprised how often that "one more" becomes the step that makes all the difference. It's like a little nudge to your confidence each time, showing you that, yes, you've got this! And that's a feeling that's worth every bit of effort. Keep it up!

●●●

한 번만 더.

상황이 힘들어져서 포기하려 할 때, 바로 그때가 한 번만 더 해 보라며 자신에게 도전해야 할 순간이야. 트랙을 한 바퀴 더 돌거나, 수학 문제를 하나 더 풀거나, 발표를 한 번 더 연습해 보거나, 어떤 것도 괜찮아. 중요한 건 처음의 '할 수 없다'라는 생각을 밀어내고, 실은 할 수 있다는 걸 알게 되는 거야.

중요한 건 지나치게 무리하는 게 아니라, 네 안에 네가 생각했던 것보다 더 많은 게 있음을 스스로에게 증명하는 거야. 넌 그 '한 번 더'가 얼마나 자주 그 모든 차이를 낳는 한 걸음이 되는지에 놀랄 거야. 그건 매번 자신감에 주는 작은 자극처럼, 네가 할 수 있다는 확신을 보여 주거든! 그리고 그 느낌은 모든 노력을 해 볼 만한 가치가 있어. 그렇게 계속 나아가!

lap 한 바퀴 | run-through 예행연습 |
overdo 지나치게 하다 | nudge 쿡 찌르다

Transform Your Mood.

You know what's a game changer for your mood and energy? Getting regular exercise. Now, I'm not saying you have to run a marathon or anything. Just find something that gets you moving and makes you happy. It could be doing air squats, hiking, or even just a walk around the block.

The key is to make it a regular part of your routine, and not just something you do once in a blue moon. It's amazing how much better you'll feel, both physically and mentally, when you stay active.

And hey, it's a great way to clear your head and de-stress too. So, go on, find that activity that makes you feel alive, and make it a must for your day. You got this!

●●●

기분을 바꿔 봐.

기분과 활력에 판도를 바꾸는 게 뭔지 알아? 규칙적으로 운동하는 거야. 지금 마라톤이나 그런 걸 뛰어야 한다는 말이 아니야. 그저 너를 움직이고 행복하게 하는 무언가를 찾으라는 거야. 스콧이나 등산을 하거나, 그냥 동네를 한 바퀴 걸어도 좋아.

핵심은 그냥 가끔 하는 게 아니라 루틴의 일부로 만드는 거야. 몸을 꾸준히 움직이면, 신체적, 정신적으로도 놀랄 만큼 활력을 느낄 거야. 머릿속도 정리되고 스트레스도 풀리는 아주 좋은 방법이야.

그러니 시작해 봐. 살아 있다고 느끼게 해 주는 활동을 찾아 하루의 필수 일과로 만들어 봐. 넌 할 수 있어!

regular 규칙적인 | air squat 스쾃 |
once in a blue moon 극히 드물게 | de-stress 스트레스를 풀다

Add Fuel to Your Growth Fire.

Imagine your personal growth as a campfire. The more wood you add, the bigger and warmer it gets. Similarly, the pace at which you grow significantly depends on how often and how much effort you put into your personal growth fire. It's really straightforward—the more time and energy you dedicate, the quicker and fuller your growth.

It's about showing up every day, even if some days are harder than others. Let's say you want to get a six-pack. If you do crunches every day, and gradually increase the number of reps you do each time, you'll have washboard abs in no time! Each effort, no matter how small, adds fuel to your fire.

It's a continuous effort, sometimes exhausting, but it's so rewarding. So, keep piling on the efforts, keep fueling your fire, and you'll see how wonderfully warm and bright it can get.

●●●

성장이라는 불에 연료를 더해 봐.

개인적인 성장을 모닥불이라고 상상해 봐. 나무를 더 많이 넣을수록 불은 더 커지고 따뜻해져. 마찬가지로 네가 성장하는 속도도 개인적인 성장이라는 불에 얼마나 자주, 많이 노력을 쏟았는지에 따라 크게 달라져. 정말 간단해. 시간과 에너지를 더 많이 바칠수록 성장은 더 빠르고 더 충만해져.

어떤 날은 더 버겁더라도, 매일 꾸준히 하는 게 중요해. 식스팩을 만들고 싶다고 해 보자. 매일 크런치를 하고 매번 반복 횟수를 조금씩 늘리면, 곧 빨래판 복근을 갖게 될 거야!

모든 노력은, 아무리 작아도 성장이라는 불에 연료를 더해 줘. 그건 끊임없는 노력으로, 때론 지치지만 무척 보람 있는 일이야. 그러니 계속 노력하고 계속 불에 연료를 더하다 보면 불이 얼마나 따뜻하고 밝아지는지 알게 될 거야.

dedicate 바치다 | crunch 크런치(누워서 몸을 반만 일으키는 상복부 운동) |
rep 반복 운동 | washboard abs 빨래판 복근 | rewarding 보람 있는

Don't Kid Yourself.

Remember, it's really easy to fool yourself. That's why it's so important to always be true to who you are. Think of honesty with yourself as a map guiding you on your journey. It keeps you on track, even when shortcuts seem tempting.

A good habit is to regularly reflect on your feelings and decisions. Like, when you're deciding on a major or a profession, ask yourself: "Do I want to do this because I genuinely like it or simply to satisfy my family's wishes?" This self-check helps you make choices that truly match your interests and values.

Every time you're honest with yourself, you're paving the way to a life that's genuinely fulfilling and authentic to who you are. Always remember to stay true to yourself—it's the best path to take!

●●●

자신을 속이지 마.

자신을 속이기는 정말 쉽다는 걸 기억해. 그게 바로 자신에게 항상 솔직해지는 게 중요한 이유야. 그 솔직함을 네 여정을 안내해 주는 지도로 생각해 봐. 지도는 지름길이 유혹할 때도 궤도를 벗어나지 않게 해 줘.

좋은 습관은 감정과 결정을 꾸준히 되돌아보는 거야. 전공이나 직업을 결정할 때 자신에게 물어봐. '이 일을 진심으로 좋아해서 하고 싶은 걸까, 아니면 단지 가족의 기대를 만족시키기 위해서일까?' 이런 자기 점검은 네 흥미와 가치에 진정으로 어울리는 선택을 하는 데 도움을 줘.

자신에게 솔직해질 때마다, 진짜 만족스럽고 너다운 삶으로 가는 길을 닦아 나가는 거야. 항상 자신에게 진실하게 살아가는 걸 잊지 마. 그게 최고의 길이니까!

reflect 반영하다 | match 어울리는, 맞는 | authentic 진짜의

Label Wisely.

To paraphrase Shakespeare, "Nothing is good or bad, but the way you think about it makes it good or bad." We have the power to give meaning to things around us. Everything's like a blank canvas, and we get to decide what color, shape, or image it holds. If you label something as bad or good, that's the reality you create for yourself. It's all in the labels, the meanings you attach.

For instance, if you label a setback as a "failure," it might bring you down. But call it a "lesson," and it will teach you something. You learn, you grow, and you're happier for it.

The labels you choose create your emotions and experiences. So, whenever you're about to label something, take a pause, and choose a label that brings positivity and growth. Your happiness truly is in your hands, or should I say, in your labels.

● ● ●

현명하게 이름 붙여.

셰익스피어의 말을 빌리자면, '좋고 나쁜 것은 없어. 다 생각하기 나름이야.' 우리는 주변 모든 것에 의미를 부여하는 힘이 있어. 모든 게 텅 빈 캔버스 같아서, 어떤 색깔이나 모양, 그림을 담을지는 우리가 결정해. 어떤 일에 좋다거나 나쁘다는 꼬리표를 붙이면, 그게 바로 자신을 위해 창조한 현실이 돼. 그 현실은 모두 네가 붙인 꼬리표, 그 의미 안에 있어.

예를 들어, 차질에 '실패'라는 꼬리표를 붙이면, 그게 널 무너뜨릴지도 몰라. 하지만 '교훈'이라고 부르면, 그게 무언가를 가르쳐 줄 거야. 그렇게 너는 배우고 성장하고 더 행복해질 거야.

네가 붙인 이름들은 감정과 경험을 창조해. 그러니 무언가에 꼬리표를 붙이려고 할 때마다, 잠시 멈춰서 긍정과 성장을 가져올 이름을 선택해. 행복은 사실 네 손안에, 아니 이렇게 말할까, 네가 붙이는 꼬리표 안에 있어.

paraphrase 바꾸어 말하다 | canvas 캔버스 |
attach 붙이다 | setback 차질

"Whenever you glance at it,
you'll have a visual nudge of the good stuff in your life."
-from Day 51-

"거기에 눈길이 닿을 때마다 삶의 좋은 것들을 보며
시각적으로 살짝 등을 떠밀릴 거야."

Gratitude Collage Keeps You Positive.

How about making a gratitude collage? Grab some photos and bits and pieces that remind you of what you're thankful for. It's like a mood board but for gratitude. Assemble them into a cool collage and hang it up where you'll see it all the time. Whenever you glance at it, you'll have a visual nudge of the good stuff in your life. It could be snaps from a trip, a ticket stub from a concert, even a doodle from your little cousin.

Seeing your personal collection of happy moments can brighten your day and keep those thankful vibes strong. It's a simple way to keep your spirits up and remember the cool things that make life sparkle.

●●●

감사 콜라주는 긍정의 마음을 지켜 줘.

감사 콜라주를 만들어 보면 어때? 감사하는 마음이 떠오르게 하는 사진과 이런저런 것들을 모아 봐. 콘셉트 보드와 비슷하지만, 감사를 위한 거야. 모은 것들을 근사한 콜라주로 만들어 언제나 보이는 곳에 걸어 두는 거지. 거기에 눈길이 닿을 때마다 삶의 좋은 것들을 보며 시각적으로 살짝 등을 떠밀릴 거야. 여행 사진, 잘린 콘서트 표, 사촌 동생이 그려준 낙서도 괜찮아.

행복한 순간을 담은 수집품을 보면 하루가 밝아지고 감사한 마음도 강하게 남아. 기분을 끌어올리고, 삶을 반짝이게 하는 멋진 일들을 기억하는 단순한 방법이야.

assemble 모으다 | glance 흘끗 보다 | snap 스냅 사진 |
doodle 낙서 | sparkle 빛나다, 생기 넘치다

Gotta Have a Plan B.

Look, not everything's gonna go the way you want it to, right? So, when you hit a wall, don't just stand there staring at it—take another route. That's where your Plan B comes in. Yeah, it's more than just a cool phrase; it's a lifesaver when things go badly.

Being flexible isn't a sign of weakness, it's actually being smart and ready for whatever life throws at you. So, if Plan A fails, don't sweat it. Adapt and move on with Plan B. It's kinda like having a spare tire in the car. You hope you never have to use it, but you're really glad it's there when you need it. Keep rolling, you got this.

●●●

플랜 B는 꼭 필요해.

모든 일이 원하는 대로 흘러가지는 않을 거야, 그렇지? 그러니 벽에 부딪혔다고 그냥 거기 서서 바라보고만 있지는 마. 다른 길을 찾아봐. 그게 바로 플랜 B가 등장할 지점이야. 맞아, 이건 단순히 멋진 구절이 아니라, 일이 꼬였을 때 너를 구해 줄 생명 줄이야. 유연하다는 게 약하다는 신호는 아니야. 오히려 현명하고, 삶이 내던지는 것들에 준비가 되어 있다는 거지. 그러니 플랜 A가 실패해도 진땀 흘리진 마. 그 사실을 받아들이고 플랜 B로 넘어가면 돼. 차에 스페어타이어를 싣고 다니는 것과 같아. 쓸 일이 없기를 바라지만 필요할 땐 그게 있어서 정말 다행이지. 계속 해, 너는 할 수 있어.

hit a wall 벽에 부딪히다 | route 길, 경로 |
lifesaver 생명의 은인 | spare tire 스페어타이어

Keep It Fresh.

Learning English should be fun and something you look forward to, not a chore. If you've tried a method for a while but it's just not clicking, don't force it. It might not be the right fit for you at this moment, and that's okay. You might find that it works better for you down the line.

The same goes for methods you used to enjoy but now find tiresome. Give yourself permission to switch things up. There are so many different ways to learn, so don't limit yourself.

The key is to keep things fresh and exciting. That way, you'll stay motivated and eager to learn more. Remember, the best method is the one that works for you right now!

● ● ●

늘 새롭게.

영어 공부는 하기 싫은 일이 아니라, 재미있고 기대되는 일이어야 해. 어떤 공부법을 한동안 시도해 봤는데 잘 맞지 않는다면, 억지로 하지 마. 지금은 너에게 맞지 않을 수도 있어. 그래도 괜찮아. 나중에 다시 시도했을 때 더 잘 맞을 수도 있으니까.

마찬가지로 예전엔 재미있었던 방법이 지금은 지루하게 느껴질 수도 있어. 자신에게 방법을 바꿔 볼 기회를 줘. 공부하는 방법은 아주 많으니, 스스로 한계를 정하지 마.

핵심은 모든 걸 늘 새롭고 재미있게 하는 거야. 그러면 계속 동기를 얻어 더 공부하고 싶어질 거야. 기억해, 바로 지금 너에게 맞는 방법이 최고의 공부법이라는 걸!

chore 하기 싫은 일, 허드렛일 | tiresome 지루한, 귀찮은 |
ermission 허락, 허가 | switch 바꾸다 | eager 간절히 바라는

Don't Just Help Others Achieve Their Dreams.

If you don't have your own goals, you'll end up working hard to help someone else achieve their dreams. And guess what? Their goals are designed to make the goal setter's life awesome, not yours.

You must have your own goals, regardless of the stage of life you're in. For instance, parents often make their goals about their children, which causes them to sacrifice their needs for their kids' needs. As a parent, be sure to have personal goals, too. That way, when your kids leave home, you won't have such an empty feeling inside.

Also, when you retire, make sure to keep setting goals so that you don't just mope around the house. For example, you're never too old to learn a new language or learn how to use the latest tech. Research shows that doing these activities increases levels of fulfillment, health, and even longevity.

With goals, you'll maintain your sense of personal dignity and experience a sense of accomplishment whenever you achieve something new.

•••

남의 꿈만 이뤄 주려 애쓰지 마.

자기만의 목표가 없다면, 결국 다른 사람이 꿈을 이루도록 열심히 돕기만 할 거야. 그리고 그거 알아? 그 목표는 네가 아니라 목표를 세운 사람의 삶을 멋지게 만들도록 설계된 거야.

인생의 어느 시기에 있든, 자신만의 목표를 가져야 해. 예를 들어, 부모들은 종종 자녀에 대한 걸 목표로 삼고, 아이들의 필요를 위해 자신의 필요를 희생하곤 해. 부모라도 개인적인 목표를 가져야 해. 그러면 자녀가 독립할 때, 마음에 공허감을 그렇게 크게 느끼지 않게 될 거야.

그리고 은퇴해서도, 집에서 그냥 맥없이 있지 않도록 계속 목표를 세워. 예를 들어, 새로운 언어를 배우거나 최신 기술을 사용하는 방법을 익히는 데는 나이 제한이 없어. 연구에 따르면 이런 활동이 만족감, 건강, 수명까지도 증가시킨다고 해.

목표와 함께, 너는 자신만의 존엄을 지키고, 새로운 무언가를 이룰 때마다 성취감을 경험할 거야.

sacrifice 희생하다 | mope 느릿느릿 움직이다, 맥없이 돌아다니다 |
longevity 수명 | dignity 존엄

Give Them the Love They Really Want.

Here's a thing about relationships that might surprise you. We sometimes think that because we've been with someone for a while, we totally get what they need. So, we start giving them what we think they should want—usually the same things we want. Seems logical, right?

But then they're not happy at all about our "gifts," and we're like, "How can you not be more grateful after all I've done for you?" Even if you ask them what they want directly, they probably won't know.

So, how do you figure it out? Simple! Just notice what they always do for you. For example, if they constantly tell you, "I love you," they need you to do the same. Alternatively, if they always hug or kiss you, that's what they need you to do, too! Wanna be happy? Give them what they truly want, and it's a done deal.

●●●

그들이 진정으로 원하는 사랑을 줘.

관계에 대한 놀라운 사실이 하나 있어. 때로 우리는 누군가와 얼마간 함께했기 때문에 그들이 뭘 필요로 하는지 모두 안다고 생각해. 그래서 그들이 원할 거로 생각하는 걸 주기 시작하지. 보통 우리가 원하는 거 말이야. 논리적인 것 같지?

하지만 그들은 우리가 준 '선물'에 전혀 행복해하지 않고, 우리는 '내가 너를 위해 이렇게까지 해 줬는데 어떻게 더 고마워하지 않을 수 있지?'라고 생각해. 직접 뭘 원하는지 물어도, 아마 그들도 모를 거야.

그럼 어떻게 알아볼까? 간단해! 그들이 항상 너에게 해 주는 게 뭔지 잘 살펴봐. 예를 들어, 네게 '사랑해'라고 끊임없이 말한다면, 그들도 같은 걸 원해. 대신, 늘 너를 안아 주거나 입 맞춘다면, 그게 바로 그들이 원하는 거야! 행복하고 싶어? 그들이 진정으로 원하는 걸 줘. 그걸로 충분해.

logical 논리적인 | directly 직접 |
constantly 끊임없이 | alternatively 대신

Swap & Conquer.

You know how sometimes you're stuck on a problem, and it just feels like you're spinning your wheels? Here's a fun twist to try out. Team up with a friend and swap a tricky challenge you're each dealing with. It's like taking a break from your own puzzle and diving into theirs. You might be surprised at how seeing their challenge from a fresh angle gives you new insights—kind of like a mental cross-training.

Plus, helping each other out? It's a double win. You both get a shot of confidence, shake off that "stuck" feeling, and flex those problem-solving muscles in a whole new way. Give it a go and watch how your grit grows—together you're stronger!

● ● ●

바꿔서 이겨 내.

어떤 문제에 갇혀서 쳇바퀴를 돌리고 있는 듯한 기분이 들 때 있지? 그럴 땐 재미있게 바꿔 봐. 친구와 짝을 이뤄 각자 겪고 있는 어려운 도전을 맞바꿔 보는 거야. 네 퍼즐을 잠시 내려놓고 친구의 퍼즐에 뛰어들어 보는 거지. 친구의 도전을 새로운 각도로 보는 데서 어떻게 새로운 통찰을 얻게 되는지, 놀랄 수도 있어. 정신적 크로스트레이닝 같은 거랄까.

게다가 서로를 돕는 거잖아? 그건 서로에게 윈윈이지. 둘 다 자신감을 한잔 들이켜고, '막막한' 기분도 털어 내고, 완전히 새로운 방식으로 문제 해결 근육을 풀어 보는 거야. 한번 시도해 보고 근성이 어떻게 자라는지 지켜봐. 함께할 때 우리는 더 강해져!

twist 변형 | insight 통찰 | **cross-training** 크로스트레이닝
(다양한 운동을 수행하는 훈련 방식) | **a shot** 한 잔

The Source of Most Happiness.

Did you know that most of your happiness in life comes from your interactions with others? So, let's talk about a simple way you can make life feel more fulfilling. Spend quality time with family and friends. It's so important to nurture those relationships because they provide a strong support system, and life's just better when you have people to share it with. Whether it's a weekend hangout, a quick chat on the phone, or even just a text to check in, make an effort to connect with your loved ones regularly. It doesn't have to be anything big or fancy— just showing that you care and are thinking about them can make a world of difference.

Plus, it's a great way to create lasting memories that you'll cherish forever. Your future self will thank you for it.

●●●

행복의 최대 원천

삶의 행복이 대부분 다른 사람들과의 소통에서 온다는 거 알아? 그러니까 삶을 더 만족스럽게 하는 간단한 방법을 이야기해 보자. 가족, 친구들과 소중한 시간을 보내도록 해. 그런 관계는 강력한 지지 기반이 되어 주기 때문에 정성껏 돌보는 게 정말 중요하거든. 그리고 삶은 함께 나눌 사람들이 있을 때 무조건 더 좋아. 주말에 만나든, 전화로 짧게 대화하든, 문자로 안부를 전하든, 사랑하는 사람들과 꾸준히 연락하려고 노력하도록 해. 크거나 거창할 필요는 없어. 그냥 그들을 소중하게 여기고 생각하고 있다는 걸 보여 주는 것만으로도 커다란 차이를 만들 수 있어.

더불어 그건 영원히 소중히 할, 오래가는 기억을 만드는 훌륭한 방식이야. 미래의 네가 지금의 너에게 고마워할 거야.

interaction 소통, 상호 작용 | fulfilling 만족스러운 | hangout 어울림 |
connect 연결하다, 연락하다 | lasting 오래 지속되는

It's a New Game with New Rules.

Have you noticed how fast everything seems to be changing these days? It's like we're on a train with no brakes, and guess what? It's not slowing down—it's speeding up.

Now, you might be winning in your areas of expertise today, but tomorrow? It could be a whole new game with new rules. That's where the fun begins! No matter how good you get, there's always a new mountain to climb, a new skill to master. And here's a cool part—you don't have to go at it alone. There's no shame in reaching out to others for some advice or help. Everyone has something to learn and something to teach.

So, when the world gives you a new challenge, grab it and grow with it. Keep your curiosity alive and keep learning. The future? It's nothing but an exciting adventure waiting to begin!

●●●

새로운 규칙이 있는 새로운 게임이야.

요즘 세상이 얼마나 빨리 변하고 있는지 눈치챘어? 마치 브레이크가 없는 기차에 타고 있는 것 같은데, 그거 알아? 속도가 줄어들지 않아. 더 빨라지고 있어.

지금은 네 전문 분야에서 앞서고 있을지도 모르지만, 내일은 어떨까? 내일은 새로운 규칙이 있는 새로운 게임이 될 수도 있어. 그게 바로 재미가 시작되는 지점이야! 아무리 능숙해져도, 항상 새로 오를 산과 새로 익혀야 할 기술이 있어. 그리고 멋진 부분이 있어. 그 길을 혼자 가지 않아도 된다는 거야. 다른 사람들에게 연락해 조언이나 도움을 청하는 건 부끄러운 일이 아니야. 모든 사람은 배울 것도 있고 가르쳐 줄 것도 있어.

그러니 세상이 새로운 도전을 내놓으면 꽉 붙잡고 함께 성장해 가는 거야. 계속 호기심을 가지고 배워 나가. 미래? 그건 곧 시작될 신나는 모험일 뿐이야.

area of expertise 전문 분야 | master 배우다, 익히다 |
shame 부끄러움, 창피 | curiosity 호기심

Me Time.

Self-love is like being your own best friend. It's about appreciating and caring for yourself just as much as you would for someone you deeply care about. This isn't just feel-good talk, either; it's about building a strong, positive relationship with yourself.

Here's a tip: set aside some "me time" every day. It can be anything that makes you feel relaxed and happy. For example, grab a massage ball (like a tennis ball) and spend 10 minutes working out the knots in your muscles. We tend to spend so much time hunched over a computer now, so a massage ball can make a huge difference in how you feel.

"Me time" is like pressing the pause button on the busy world around you and focusing on your inner peace. This practice helps you reconnect with yourself and reminds you that you're important. Remember, when you love and respect yourself, you're teaching the world how to love and respect you too. Keep glowing!

● ● ●

나만의 시간

자기애는 자신에게 가장 좋은 친구가 되어 주는 것과 같아. 네가 소중하게 여기는 사람에게 하는 만큼, 자신을 인정하고 보살피는 거야. 단지 기분 좋아지는 말이 아니야. 중요한 건 자기 자신과 강하고 긍정적인 관계를 맺는 거야.

팁을 하나 줄게. 매일 '나만의 시간'을 마련해 봐. 편안해지고 행복해지는 어떤 걸 해도 좋아. 예를 들어, 마사지 볼(테니스공 같은)을 이용해 10분간 뭉친 근육을 풀어 주는 거야. 요즘 우리는 너무 오래 컴퓨터 앞에서 등을 구부리고 있는 경향이 있어서 마사지 볼이 네 기분에 엄청난 차이를 만들 수 있어.

'나만의 시간'은 주변의 바쁜 세상에 일시 정지 버튼을 누르고 내면의 평화에 집중하는 것이나 마찬가지야. 이런 연습은 자신과 다시 연결되고, 자신이 중요하다는 걸 다시금 떠오르게 해. 잊지 마, 너 자신을 사랑하고 존중할 때, 세상에도 널 사랑하고 존중하는 법을 가르쳐 주는 거야. 늘 반짝이길!

massage 마사지 | knot 뻣뻣함, 매듭 |
reconnect 다시 연결되다

Your Journey, Your Pace.

Just a little reminder: it's totally okay that everyone grows and learns at their own pace. You might see some friends picking up things faster or reaching their goals quickly, but that's their journey, not yours. You have your own unique path, and that's what's important. It's like flowers in a garden; they don't all blossom at the same rate, and that's the beauty of nature.

So, don't worry if you feel like you're moving a bit slower. How about you set goals based on your rate of progress and celebrate your small wins? Whether it's understanding a tough concept or just making it through a challenging day, acknowledging these moments can really boost your confidence.

Remember, you can't rush growth. Just like a rose needs time to bloom, you need time to grow in your own special way. Keep going at your pace, and you'll see how wonderfully you progress. You're doing amazing!

●●●

너의 여정, 너의 속도

기억할 게 하나 있어. 모두가 자신만의 속도로 성장하고 배워도 정말 괜찮다는 거야. 어떤 친구들은 더 빨리 배우거나 더 빨리 목표에 도달할지도 모르지만, 그건 그들의 여정이지, 네 것이 아니야. 너에겐 너만의 길이 있고, 그게 중요한 거야. 정원에 있는 꽃들과 마찬가지야. 꽃들도 모두 같은 속도로 피지 않고, 그게 바로 자연의 아름다움이야.

그러니 조금 더 느리게 가는 것 같아도 걱정하지 마. 네 진행 속도에 맞춰 목표를 정하고 소소한 성취를 축하해 주면 어떨까? 어려운 개념을 이해한 거든, 힘든 하루를 버텨낸 거든, 이런 순간들을 인정하면 자신감이 정말 커질 거야.

성장을 재촉할 수는 없다는 걸 기억하도록 해. 장미가 피려면 시간이 필요하듯, 너만의 특별한 방식으로 성장하려면 시간이 필요해. 계속 너의 속도로 가다 보면 네가 얼마나 멋지게 나아가고 있는지 알게 될 거야. 넌 잘하고 있어!

rate 속도 | concept 개념 | bloom 꽃이 피다

Phase 7

Embrace Results

결과 받아들이기

"The progress will show itself in time. And when it does,
you'll be amazed at how much you've grown."
-from Day 63-

"시간이 지나면 그 진전이 드러날 거야. 그리고 그때,
네가 얼마나 많이 자랐는지 깜짝 놀랄 거야."

Gratitude Walks.

How about you make your daily walks (or commutes, or errand runs, or any other time you're traveling) a bit more interesting? Next time, find something around you, anything really, that you feel grateful for. Maybe, it's the cool breeze, the sound of leaves rustling, or even the irregular shapes of clouds in the sky.

It's all about noticing the little things that make your world beautiful. Doing this, you're not just getting your steps in; you're connecting with the world around you on a whole new level. It's pretty amazing how just looking for things to appreciate can totally change your vibe and make you feel more grounded.

So, lace up, step out, and turn a simple walk into a journey of gratitude. It's a small change that can make a big difference in how you see the world.

● ● ●

감사 걷기

매일의 산책(혹은 출퇴근길이나 심부름하거나 다른 이동하는 시간)을 조금 더 흥미롭게 만들어 보는 건 어때? 다음번엔 주변에서 감사할 만한 무언가를, 정말 무엇이든 찾아봐. 어쩌면 시원한 산들바람이나 바스락거리는 나뭇잎 소리, 하늘에 떠 있는 모양이 제각각인 구름일 수도 있어.

중요한 건 세상을 아름답게 하는 자그마한 것들을 깨닫는 거야. 이렇게 하다 보면, 걸음 수를 채울 뿐 아니라 주변 세상과 완전히 새로운 차원으로 연결될 거야. 정말 놀라운 건 감사할 것들을 찾는 것만으로도, 얼마나 기분이 달라지고 차분해지는지야.

그러니 신발 끈을 매고, 밖으로 나가, 단순한 걷기를 감사의 여정으로 바꿔 봐. 세상을 보는 눈에 커다란 차이를 만들 수 있는 작은 변화야.

breeze 산들바람 | rustle 바스락거리다 | irregular 불규칙적인 |
grounded 균형 잡힌 | lace up 신발 끈을 묶다

Pause a Moment and Everything Changes.

When you feel like everything is coming at you all at once, sometimes the best thing you can do is just pause for a moment. I'm not saying you should run away from your problems, but give yourself a short, 10-minute break. You could meditate, go for a brisk walk, or even take a power nap. The idea is to step back, gain a new perspective, and let your mind refresh itself.

When you return to whatever challenge you're facing, you'll find yourself much more equipped to handle it. It's like when a computer starts to slow down— sometimes all it needs is a quick restart to work more efficiently.

So, don't hesitate to give yourself a little time-out. It can truly make a world of difference.

●●●

잠시 멈추면 모든 게 달라져.

모든 일이 한꺼번에 들이닥치는 듯할 때, 때로 할 수 있는 가장 좋은 일은 그냥 잠시 멈추는 거야. 문제에서 도망치라는 말이 아니라, 짧게, 10분의 휴식을 취하라는 거야. 명상하거나, 활기차게 걷거나, 짧게 낮잠을 자도 좋아. 요점은 한 걸음 물러나 새로운 시각을 얻고 마음에 생기를 되찾는 거야.

다시 도전으로 돌아왔을 때는, 닥친 일에 대처할 준비를 더 잘 갖춘 자신을 발견하게 될 거야. 컴퓨터가 느려지기 시작할 때의 상황과 같아. 때로는 빨리 재시작해서 더 잘 작동하도록 하는 게 필요한 전부야.

그러니 망설이지 말고, 스스로에게 짧은 중간 휴식을 주도록 해. 그게 정말 커다란 차이를 만들 수도 있어.

meditate 명상하다 | brisk 활기찬 | power nap 기력 회복을 위한 짧은 낮잠 |
equipped 장비를 갖춘 | handle 대처하다, 다루다

A Watched Pot Never Boils.

Sometimes, progress is like a sneaky little ninja—you don't see it happening, but it's there. Even when you feel like you've hit a plateau and your English isn't getting any better, trust me, it is. It's just that the results are hiding from you.

Remember the old saying that "A watched pot never boils"? Whatever you do, don't constantly check to see if you're making progress. You could be spending that precious time practicing and learning. In fact, the less you care about instant improvement and the more you simply enjoy the process, the faster you'll progress. Then, once you look back, you'll see just how far you've come.

So, if you're feeling stuck or like you're not improving, don't let that get to you. Just keep at it, keep practicing, and keep learning. The progress will show itself in time. And when it does, you'll be amazed at how much you've grown. So, chin up, believe in yourself, and charge on! You've got this!

•••

지켜보고 있는 냄비는 절대 끓지 않아.

발전은 때로 교활한 작은 닌자 같아. 나타나는 게 보이지 않지만, 거기 있어. 정체기에 부딪혀 영어 실력이 더 나아지고 있지 않는 것 같을 때도, 사실 나아지고 있어. 그저 결과가 숨어 있을 뿐이야.

'지켜보고 있는 냄비는 절대 끓지 않는다'라는 옛말 기억해? 뭘 하든 앞으로 나아가고 있는지 끊임없이 확인하지 마. 연습하고 배울 귀중한 시간을 버리고 있을 수도 있어. 사실, 즉각적인 성과에 덜 집착하고, 단순히 그 과정을 더 즐길수록 더 빨리 발전할 거야. 그리고 문득 뒤를 돌아봤을 때 얼마나 멀리 왔는지 깨닫게 될 거야.

그러니 막막하거나 나아지지 않는 듯 느껴져도 실망하지 마. 그냥 계속 해, 계속 연습하고 계속 배워. 시간이 지나면 그 진전이 드러날 거야. 그리고 그때, 네가 얼마나 많이 자랐는지 깜짝 놀랄 거야. 그러니 기운 내고, 자신을 믿고, 앞으로 돌격! 넌 할 수 있어!

sneaky 교활한 | ninja 닌자 | plateau 정체기 | chin up 기운 내다

Continually Celebrate, Continually Advance.

When you're hustling towards a goal, don't forget to give yourself some credit for what you've already achieved. Yes, even for those little victories! They don't just make you feel good; they actually get your brain to seek out more wins. It's like positive feedback for your mental state.

But you need to be careful, too—don't get too caught up living in your past victories. Most of your focus should be on the road ahead.

So, after you've done your celebrations, get right back into it. No one ever became great by just sitting around, high fiving themselves. You gotta earn those high fives by crushing what's next. So, go on, take a moment to celebrate, but then get right back to making things happen. Trust me, you won't regret it.

●●●

끊임없이 축하하고, 끊임없이 나아가.

목표를 향해 밀고 나갈 때, 이미 이뤄 낸 일에 대해 자신을 인정해 주는 걸 잊지 마. 맞아, 아주 작은 성공이라도! 그건 기분을 좋게 할 뿐 아니라, 실제로 뇌가 더 많은 성공을 찾아내도록 해. 마치 마음의 상태에 주는 긍정적인 피드백 같은 거야.

하지만 주의할 필요도 있어. 과거의 성공 속에 머물러 있지는 마. 대부분의 초점을 앞에 있는 길에 맞춰야 해.

그러니 축하한 다음에는 곧장 돌아가. 그냥 가만히 앉아 자신과 하이 파이브 하며 위대해진 사람은 없어. 다음 목표를 뭉개 버리는 걸로 하이 파이브를 얻어 내야 해. 그러니 해 봐, 잠시 축하하되, 그다음엔 목표를 이루기 위해 바로 되돌아가는 거야. 날 믿어, 후회하지 않을 테니.

hustle 밀치다 | credit 칭찬, 인정 | high five 하이 파이브 | crush 뭉개다

Don't Take Them for Granted.

Whatever you do, never take your loved ones for granted. Life gets busy, schedules get packed, but no matter how busy we get, we crave connection, love, and understanding. The people who stand by us, through the ups and downs, are the true treasures of our lives. It's easy to think they'll always be there, especially when the days seem to blur together.

But it's important to pause, appreciate their presence, and express our gratitude. Small things, such as a thank you note, a chat over bubble tea, or a simple hug can mean the world to them. It's about making sure they know how much they mean to you, and never missing a chance to show them love and appreciation. It's the little things that maintain and strengthen your bond, making life sweeter along the way.

•••

당연하게 여기지 마.

무슨 일이 있어도 사랑하는 이들을 당연하게 여기지 마. 삶이 분주하고 일정이 빡빡해도, 얼마나 바쁘건 상관없이, 우리는 관계와 사랑, 이해를 갈망해. 기쁠 때나 슬플 때나 곁을 지켜 주는 사람들은 삶의 진정한 보물이야. 그들이 늘 거기 있을 거로 생각하기는 쉬워. 하루하루가 비슷하게 흘러가다 보면 특히 그래.

그래서 잠시 멈춰, 그들의 존재에 감사하고 그 감사를 표현하는 게 중요해. 감사 편지, 버블티를 마시며 나누는 대화, 단순한 포옹 같은 작은 것들이 그들에게는 더없이 중요한 의미일 수도 있어. 그들이 너에게 얼마나 큰 의미인지 알려 주고, 그들에게 사랑과 감사를 표현할 기회를 절대 놓치지 마. 그런 작은 것들이 유대를 유지하고 강하게 하며, 그 과정에서 삶을 더 달콤하게 해.

crave 갈망하다, 열망하다 | connection 관계, 연결 | blur 흐릿해지다

Show Yourself You Can Tackle Challenges.

Start your day by picking one thing that's a bit of a challenge for you. Make it your mission to take it head-on first thing. See, when you dive into that challenge with fresh morning energy, you're setting yourself up for a win straight off the bat.

It's not just about getting it out of the way—it's about proving to yourself that you've got what it takes to face the hard stuff. And trust me, that feeling of nailing it? That's going to fuel your confidence and keep you going strong all day.

So, choose your challenge, roll up your sleeves, and show that task who's boss. Here's to making perseverance your secret weapon and every morning your victory lap!

●●●

도전에 맞설 수 있다는 걸 스스로에게 보여 줘.

조금 어려운 일을 하나 고르는 걸로 하루를 시작해 봐. 가장 먼저 그 일에 정면으로 부딪치는 걸 그날의 임무로 삼는 거야. 아침의 신선한 에너지로 도전에 뛰어들 때, 너는 그 즉시 승리를 준비하는 거야.

중요한 건 단순히 일을 처리하는 게 아니라, 그 어려운 문제를 마주할 능력이 자신에게 있다는 걸 증명하는 거야. 그리고, 그걸 해내는 기분? 그건 자신감을 북돋우고 강인하게 하루를 살게 해.

그러니 도전을 선택하고, 팔을 걷어붙이고, 누가 그 일의 주인인지 보여 줘. 인내를 비밀 무기로 삼아 매일 아침을 승리의 장으로 만들어 봐!

dive into ~로 뛰어들다 | task 일 | perseverance 인내

Good Vibes Bowl.

Here's a simple but powerful idea. Take any bowl and put it where you usually chill or work. Whenever something cool happens, scribble it down on a piece of paper and pop it into the bowl. It can be really small wins, like getting a test question correct, or something big, like a long-awaited promotion.

Then, when the bowl's getting full or you're feeling blue, take out those notes and read them. You'll be surprised how much good stuff happens that you might otherwise forget. It's a great way to keep your spirits up and remember the happy times, especially when you need a boost.

Try it—you'll feel great seeing that bowl of happiness grow!

•••

좋은 기운을 담는 그릇

단순하지만 강력한 아이디어가 있어. 아무 그릇이나 꺼내서 보통 쉬거나 일하는 곳에 놓아둬. 멋진 일이 생길 때마다 작은 종이에 적어 그릇에 넣는 거야. 시험 문제 하나를 맞힌 것처럼 정말 작은 성취나 오랫동안 기다린 승진처럼 큰일도 좋아.

그리고 그릇이 거의 찼을 때나 우울할 때면 그 메모들을 꺼내서 읽어 봐. 그냥 지나쳤다면 잊혔을 좋은 일들이 얼마나 많이 일어나는지 깜짝 놀랄 거야. 특히 위로가 필요할 때, 기분을 끌어올리고 행복한 순간들을 기억하는 훌륭한 방법이야.

시도해 봐. 그 행복 그릇이 차오르는 걸 보며 기분이 아주 좋아질 거야.

good vibe 좋은 기분 | chill 쉬다 | scribble 갈겨쓰다 | pop into 넣다

If You Want to Overcome a Blind Spot, Embrace Different Perspectives.

You know, we all have our blind spots, areas of our thinking or behavior that we just can't see clearly. It's like having some dirt on your face that you don't notice until someone points it out. This is one way the people around us can help us. They can point out our blind spots, not to criticize us, but to help us see things more clearly. It's a teamwork of sorts, where we rely on others to reveal our weak spots.

So, when someone points out a blind spot, don't get defensive. Thank them for helping you to see better. It's like having an extra pair of eyes helping you navigate through life. Embrace it, learn from it, and use it to grow.

Ideally, don't wait for someone to come to you—go to them. Actively ask others what they think you could do to improve certain areas of your life or work.

●●●

맹점을 극복하고 싶다면 다른 시각을 받아들여.

우리에게는 모두 맹점이라는, 명확하게 볼 수 없는 생각이나 행동의 영역이 있어. 얼굴에 묻은 때처럼 누군가 지적해 줄 때까지 알아차리지 못해. 이게 주변 사람들이 우리를 도와줄 수 있는 한 가지 방법이야. 그들은 우리의 맹점을 짚어 줄 수 있어, 우리를 비판하려는 게 아니라 우리가 그것들을 더 확실히 볼 수 있게 도와주기 위해서야. 일종의 협업으로, 자신의 약점을 알아내려고 서로에게 의지하는 거야.

그러니 누군가 맹점을 지적할 때 방어적으로 반응하지 마. 더 잘 보게 도와준 데 감사하도록 해. 그건 삶을 항해하는 데 필요한 여분의 눈 한 쌍을 얻은 셈이야. 그 지적을 받아들이고, 그걸 배우고, 성장하는 데 활용해 봐.

이상적인 건 누군가가 다가오기를 기다리지 않는 거야. 먼저 다가가. 삶이나 일의 특정 영역을 발전시키기 위해 네가 할 수 있는 일이 무엇인지, 다른 이들에게 적극적으로 물어봐.

blind spot 맹점 | dirt 때, 흙 | defensive 방어적인

Silence the Inner Critic.

Hey, you know being too hard on yourself with self-criticism is like having a downer soundtrack in your mind. It doesn't really help; it just makes you more stressed. It's like trying to make something cool in pottery class while a voice keeps nagging that you're doing it wrong.

Try this: when you start being tough on yourself, pause and think, "Would I say this to my best friend?" Like, if you mess up and think, "I'm a failure," stop and ask yourself if you'd ever say that to a friend. You'd probably say, "Mistakes happen, let's fix it."

This friend-test changes how you talk to yourself, from criticism to support. It's like giving yourself a little pep talk. Remember, always be as kind to yourself as you would to a friend. You deserve it!

● ● ●

내면의 비평가를 잠재워.

자기비판으로 자신을 너무 엄격하게 대하면, 마음속에 우울한 사운드트랙을 틀어 놓는 거나 다름없어. 도움이 되기는커녕 스트레스만 더 받게 될 뿐이지. 도예 수업에서 근사한 작품을 만들려고 하는데, 어떤 목소리가 계속해서 잘못하고 있다고 잔소리하는 것과 같아.

그럴 땐 이렇게 해 봐. 스스로에게 엄격하게 굴려고 할 때, 잠시 멈춰 '내가 친한 친구에게도 이런 말을 할까?' 하고 생각해 봐. 마찬가지로, 실수하고 나서 '나는 실패작이야'라는 생각이 들면, 생각을 멈추고 그런 말을 친구에게도 할지 자신에게 물어봐. 너는 아마 '실수할 수도 있지, 다시 해 보자'라고 할 거야.

이 친구 테스트는 자신에게 말하는 방식을 비판에서 지지로 바꿔 줘. 마치 자신에게 작은 격려의 말을 하는 것과 같아. 기억해, 친구에게 하는 것처럼 자신에게도 늘 친절을 베풀어. 넌 그럴 자격이 있어.

soundtrack 사운드트랙 | pottery 도자기, 도예 |
nag 잔소리하다 | pep talk 격려의 말

Take the Behind-the-Scenes View.

Just a thought to share: when you see someone's success or those perfect social media posts, remember, it's just part of the story. It's like admiring a beautiful painting but not seeing the artist's hours (or weeks or months) of work.

Most successes, even those that seem overnight, are actually years in the making. Like an internet celebrity you might admire—if you check out their early work, it's often not great. They've grown through working on their craft, not just good luck. And about Instagram, it's easy to get dazzled by those ideal snapshots, but they're just highlights, not the full picture.

So, next time you feel a bit envious, remember everyone's showing their best moments. Instead of wishing you had what they have, focus on your own path, with all its unique challenges and victories. Your journey is just as important and beautiful. Keep crafting your story, step by step. You'll be astonished with the results!

•••

무대 뒤의 모습을 봐.

공유할 생각 하나: 누군가의 성공이나 완벽한 소셜 미디어 포스트를 볼 때, 그건 그 이야기의 한 부분일 뿐이라는 걸 기억해. 그건 아름다운 그림에 감탄하면서도 예술가가 들인 몇 시간(혹은 몇 주나 몇 달)은 보지 못하는 것과 같아.

대부분 성공은, 하룻밤 만에 이뤄진 듯 보여도, 사실은 수년 동안 만들어진 거야. 네가 동경할지도 모르는 인터넷 스타도 마찬가지야. 그들의 초기 작품을 확인해 보면 그다지 훌륭하지 않은 경우가 많아. 그들은 그냥 운이 좋았던 게 아니라 기술을 갈고닦으며 성장해 온 거야. 그리고 인스타그램에 대해 말하자면, 그런 이상적인 사진에 현혹되기는 쉽지만, 그건 삶 전체가 아니라 단지 하이라이트일 뿐이야.

그러니 다음에 조금 부럽게 느껴지면, 기억해. 모든 사람이 자기 최고의 순간만을 보여 준다는 걸. 그들이 가진 걸 부러워하는 대신, 특별한 도전과 승리가 있는 너만의 길에 집중해 봐. 네 여정도 그만큼 중요하고 아름다워. 네 이야기를 한 단계 한 단계 계속 만들어 가. 그 결과에 깜짝 놀랄 거야!

internet celebrity 인터넷 스타 | craft 기술, 정교하게 만들다 |
dazzle 눈부시게 하다, 현혹시키다 | envious 부러워하는 | astonished 깜짝 놀라게 하다

8

Reflect on Outcomes

결과를 되돌아보기

"So, why wait for a particular moment
to feel happy?"
-from Day 74-

"그런데 대체 왜 행복해지려고
어떤 특별한 순간을 기다리는 거지?"

The Positivity of the Miracle Magnet.

Life has its own way of tossing curveballs, but among all that, there's a cool little force at work—gratitude.

Picture your heart as a magnet. Now, the more gratitude it holds, the stronger it becomes at attracting good stuff, or as I like to call them, "miracles." It's not about the grand gestures, but the small daily acknowledgments. Being thankful for a meal, for friendship, for a roof over your head—these are the things that empower that magnet.

And before you know it, you start noticing "miracles"—unexpected, good things popping up here and there. It's like sending out positive energy into the universe that says, "Hey, I appreciate what I have," and the universe responds back by throwing a little more goodness your way. So, fill up on gratitude, and watch how life turns into this cool journey of collecting miracles.

●●●

기적을 끌어당기는 긍정이라는 자석

삶은 예상치 못한 일을 던져 주는 자기만의 방식이 있지만, 그중에서도, 작지만 멋지게 작용하는 힘이 있어. 바로 감사야.

마음을 자석이라고 상상해 봐. 그 안에 감사를 더 많이 담을수록, 좋은 것들, 혹은 내 표현대로 하자면 '기적'을 더 강하게 끌어당기게 돼. 중요한 건 거창한 몸짓이 아니라 매일의 작은 인정이야. 식사에, 우정에, 집에 감사하는 것, 이런 것들이 자석에 힘을 실어 주는 거지.

그리고 너도 모르는 사이에, 여기저기에서 튀어나오는 예상치 못한 좋은 것들, 즉 '기적'을 알아차리기 시작해. 마치 우주에 '내가 가진 것에 감사해'라고 말하는 긍정적인 에너지를 보내면, 네가 가는 길에 조금 더 축복을 건네는 걸로 우주가 대답해 주는 것과 같아. 그러니 마음을 감사로 가득 채우고, 삶이 어떻게 기적을 수집하는 멋진 여정으로 바뀌는지 지켜봐.

force 힘 | picture 그리다 | grand gesture 거창한 몸짓 | empower 힘을 실어 주다

Don't Face Problems Alone.

You know those moments when life's really hard and you feel like you're facing the world alone? Don't let that happen, alright? Seriously.

There's absolutely no shame in getting some fresh eyes on your problem. Text a friend or maybe even a relative you trust. Just let it all out. You won't believe how much a simple conversation can change your viewpoint. It's like turning on the lights in a dark room—you suddenly see things you didn't before. Maybe your friend doesn't have the perfect solution, but they might ask a question that sparks a lightbulb moment for you. The more brains in the game, the better, especially when you're stuck.

So, don't hesitate—send someone a message. Sound good?

●●●

문제에 혼자 맞서지 마.

삶이 정말 버거워서 혼자 세상과 맞서고 있는 듯 느껴지는 그런 순간, 알지? 그런 일이 일어나게 두지 마, 알겠어? 정말이야.

네 문제에 새로운 시각을 구하는 데 창피할 건 전혀 없어. 믿을 수 있는 친구나 친척에게라도 문자를 보내 봐. 그냥 다 속 시원히 말해 봐. 단순한 대화가 네 관점을 얼마나 많이 바꿀 수 있는지 믿기지 않을 거야. 어두운 방에 불을 켜는 것과 같아. 전에는 보이지 않았던 것들이 갑자기 보이게 될 거야. 친구에게 완벽한 해결책이 없을지도 모르지만, 불현듯 좋은 생각이 떠오르게 하는 질문을 할지도 몰라. 특히 꽉 막혔을 때는 게임에 참여하는 두뇌가 많을수록 더 좋아.

그러니 주저하지 마. 누군가에게 메시지를 보내. 어때?

shame 수치심, 창피 | viewpoint 관점 | hesitate 주저하다

Move Beyond the Korean-Only Definition.

Try not to lean too much on English-Korean dictionaries. Why? Well, relying on translations can make you over-dependent on Korean, thinking a few Korean meanings fully capture an English word.

But remember, English words often have more than one meaning, and English and Korean don't always align perfectly in usage and connotations. Also, English-Korean dictionaries oversimplify things, limiting your chance to truly master English. So, to really get good at English, you need to step out of the mindset of just knowing the Korean equivalent. Look at English-English dictionaries to see the full picture of a word, its various uses, and example sentences.

Also, don't hesitate to use technology for help. A quick internet search or even AI can offer explanations and examples. It's all about using every tool to learn effectively and make English truly yours. Dive into this journey and watch your language skills grow!

●●●

한국어 정의를 넘어서.

영한사전에 너무 많이 기대지 않도록 해. 왜냐고? 번역문에 의지하다 보면 한국어 의미 몇 가지가 영어 단어를 완전히 담아냈다고 생각하며 한국어에 너무 의존할 수 있거든.

하지만 기억해, 영어 단어에는 종종 의미가 하나 이상 있고, 영어와 한국어는 사용법과 함축된 의미가 항상 완벽하게 같은 선상에 있지는 않다는 걸. 게다가 영한사전은 단어의 의미를 지나치게 단순화해서 진짜 영어를 배우는 기회를 제한해. 그러니 영어를 정말 잘하기 위해서는 단어의 한국어 뜻만 알면 된다는 마음가짐에서 벗어나야 해. 단어의 전체적인 의미와 다양한 쓰임, 예문을 보려면 영영사전을 살펴봐. 또한 과학 기술을 활용해 도움받기를 주저하지 마. 간단한 인터넷 검색이나 AI로도 설명과 예시를 찾을 수 있어.

중요한 건 모든 도구를 활용해 효과적으로 배우고, 영어를 진짜 네 것으로 만드는 거야. 이 여정에 뛰어들어 언어 실력이 자라나는 걸 지켜봐!

lean on ~에 기대다 | connotation 함축된 의미 |
oversimplify 지나치게 단순화하다 | equivalent 동의어

Happiness Shouldn't Be Conditional.

You're now working toward your goals, which is awesome, but there's a common trap: putting conditions on your happiness. "I'll be happy when I get that job." "I'll be happy when I ace that test." "I'll be happy when I find true love."

As important as goals are, happiness isn't waiting at the end of some distant goal. It's right here, in this moment. It's in the smell of your morning coffee, the laughter shared with a friend, and the friendly smile of a neighbor.

When you base your joy on the "whens" and the "ifs," you miss out on the simple pleasures sitting right under your nose. So, why wait for a particular moment to feel happy? Invite joy into the ordinary, the everyday. After all, happiness is not a destination, but a way of traveling on the way to your destination.

•••

행복이 조건부여서는 안 돼.

너는 지금 목표를 향해 노력하고 있고, 그건 멋진 일이지만, 흔히 빠지는 함정이 하나 있어. 바로 행복에 조건을 붙이는 거야. '그 일을 하게 되면 행복할 거야.', '시험을 통과하면 행복할 거야.', '진정한 사랑을 찾는다면 행복할 거야.'

물론 목표도 중요하지만, 행복은 저 먼 목표의 끝에서 기다리고 있지 않아. 그건 바로 여기, 이 순간에 있어. 모닝커피 향기에, 친구와 나누는 웃음에, 이웃의 상냥한 미소에 있어.

커다란 행복을 '언제'와 '만약'에 기반을 두면, 눈앞에 있는 소박한 즐거움을 놓치게 돼. 그런데 대체 왜 행복해지려고 어떤 특별한 순간을 기다리는 거지? 행복을 평범한 일상으로 초대하도록 해. 결국, 행복은 목적지가 아니라 목적지로 가는 길 위를 나아가는 방식이야.

condition 조건 | distant 먼 | base on 기반을 두다 | particular 특정한

Forever Fill Your Relationship with Warmth.

It's a weird but common habit—showing our best selves to the outside world while being in a bad mood when we're around those closest to us. We must reverse this habit.

The people closest to you, especially your other half, deserve the best version of you. It's with them that you should exercise patience, kindness, and understanding the most. Others may come and go, but your loved ones are there long term. If you're constantly irritable or impatient towards your partner, over time, it can cause problems in your relationship.

So, make a conscious effort to be gentle, to listen, and to show appreciation to the person who matters most. Your relationship will then have the chance to blossom, and your life will be filled with a warmth that no amount of pleasing outsiders could equal.

●●●

언제나 따뜻함으로 관계를 채워 줘.

이상하지만 흔한 습관이 하나 있어. 바깥세상에는 가장 좋은 모습만 보여 주면서 정작 가장 가까운 사람들 앞에서는 나쁜 기분을 드러내는 거야. 반드시 이 습관을 뒤집어야 해.

가장 가까운 사람들, 특히 배우자는 네 가장 좋은 모습을 대할 자격이 있어. 그들과 함께일 때, 인내와 친절, 이해를 가장 많이 연습해야 해. 다른 사람들은 왔다가 갈 수도 있지만, 사랑하는 이들은 오랫동안 거기 있어. 끊임없이 배우자에게 짜증을 내거나 조급하게 군다면, 시간이 흐르면서 관계에 문제가 생길 수 있어.

그러니 의식적으로 노력해서, 가장 소중한 그 사람에게 상냥하게 대하고, 귀 기울이고, 감사를 보여 줘. 그러면 관계는 꽃이 피는 기회를 얻고, 삶은 남을 만족시키는 거로는 채울 수 없는 온기로 가득 찰 거야.

DATE _______ / _______ / _______

our best selves 최고의 모습 | reverse 뒤집다, 뒤바꾸다 | irritable 짜증 내는

A Phrase to Make You Unshakable.

Imagine having a secret phrase, like a magic spell, that boosts your strength whenever you hit a bump in the road. Sounds good? You can make one!

It's your very own "Stay Strong Phrase"—a mantra that's all about your unshakable spirit. Craft it from words that get your heart pumping with courage. Then, whenever a challenge tries to knock you down, say your mantra out loud. Let those words be the echo in your mind that drowns out the noise of doubt. It's like your inner cheerleader, reminding you that you've got what it takes to muscle through anything.

And believe me, that little echo? It can move mountains within you. Keep at it, and you'll see—you're unstoppable!

•••

네가 흔들리지 않게 해 줄 구절

마법 주문 같은 비밀 구절이 있어서 길에서 장애물에 부딪힐 때마다 힘이 솟아난다고 상상해 봐. 멋지지? 직접 하나 만들어 봐!

그게 너만의 '힘이 나는 구절', 즉 흔들림 없는 내면을 위한 만트라야. 심장이 용기로 뛰게 하는 단어들로 정성스레 만들어 봐. 그리고 어려움이 너를 쓰러뜨리려 할 때, 네 만트라를 소리 내어 말해 봐. 그 단어들이 마음속에서 메아리가 되어 의심의 소리를 잠재워 줘. 그건 내면의 치어리더처럼, 너에게 무언가를 헤치고 나아가는 데 필요한 힘이 있다는 걸 상기시켜 줄 거야.

그리고 그 작은 메아리? 그게 네 안의 산을 움직일 수 있어. 계속 되뇌다 보면 알게 될 거야. 무엇도 널 막을 수 없어!

magic spell 마법 주문 | bump 돌기, 장애물 | mantra 만트라(불교의 진언, 기도나 명상할 때 사용하는 신성한 소리와 구절) | craft 공들여 만들다 | drown out ~을 들리지 않게 하다

Unplug to Recharge.

Imagine your mind as being like a phone battery—it needs to recharge, not just at night but during the day, too.

Start with carving out little "no-phone zones" in your day. Maybe during meals, swap scrolling for actual chatting or savoring the taste of your food. Or try leaving your phone behind when you walk the dog—let your thoughts and senses roam free instead. And how about we replace just 30 minutes of screen time with something super fun offline each evening? Could be shooting hoops, reading, or cooking.

You'll probably notice more about your day, your mood might lift, and you'll definitely sleep better. It's all about giving your brain different things to do so it can stay happy and fresh. Give it a shot, and you'll be surprised how good you feel!

● ● ●

재충전하려면 플러그를 뽑아.

마음을 휴대 전화 배터리라고 상상해 봐. 밤에만이 아니라 낮에도 재충전이 필요해.

하루 중에 작은 '휴대 전화 금지 구역'을 만들어 두는 것부터 시작해. 식사 중에 스크롤 하는 대신 대화하거나 음식의 맛을 음미해 봐. 아니면 반려견을 산책시킬 때 휴대 전화를 놔두고 나가 봐. 대신 생각과 감각이 자유롭게 돌아다니게 둬. 매일 저녁 30분만, 화면 보는 시간을 굉장히 재미있는 오프라인 활동으로 바꿔 보면 어때? 농구나 독서, 요리도 좋아.

그렇게 하면 아마 하루를 더 잘 인식하게 될 거고, 기분이 좋아질 수도 있어. 분명히 잠도 더 잘 올 거야. 핵심은 뇌에 다른 할 일을 주는 거야. 그러면 마음을 행복하고 생기있게 유지할 수 있어. 한번 해 봐, 얼마나 기분이 좋아지는지 놀라게 될 거야.

carve out 자르다 | zone 구역 | scroll 스크롤 하다, 화면을 넘기다 | roam 돌아다니다

A You That's Ready to Go.

You know, sometimes you may find yourself in a job that doesn't excite you. That's a common situation, but it doesn't have to be a permanent one. In fact, the benefit of that kind of job is the room for growth.

Instead of letting the dissatisfaction grow out of control, use it as motivation to work on yourself. This is your big chance to learn new skills, improve existing ones, or even explore entirely new fields. The aim is to turn yourself into someone qualified for a job you'd love. It's all about upping your game, so that when opportunity knocks, it will see that you are ready and worthy.

Remember, every step you take towards self-improvement is a step closer to a job that makes you jump out of bed in the morning!

•••

나설 준비가 된 너

때로 설레지 않는 일을 하고 있는 자신을 발견할지도 몰라. 흔한 상황이지만, 그게 영원할 필요는 없어. 사실, 그런 일의 장점은 성장할 여지가 있다는 거야.

불만이 통제 불능으로 커지게 두지 말고, 자신을 발전시키는 동기로 활용하도록 해. 새로운 기술을 배우거나, 기존 기술을 향상하거나, 완전히 새로운 분야를 탐색해 볼 수도 있는 절호의 기회야. 목표는 하고 싶은 일을 할 자격이 있는 사람으로 자신을 바꾸는 거야. 중요한 건 실력을 끌어올려, 기회가 문을 두드릴 때, 네가 준비되어 있고 가치 있다는 걸 보여 주는 거야.

기억해, 자기 향상을 향해 내딛는 한 걸음 한 걸음이 아침에 이불을 박차고 나오게 만들 직업에 가까워지는 한 걸음이야.

dissatisfaction 불만 | explore 탐험하다 |
qualified 자격이 있는 | worthy 가치가 있는

Don't Inhibit Your Emotions.

You know, it's totally okay to let your emotions out sometimes. As we grow up, we often learn to keep our feelings under wraps, especially in public. We think we're being strong by not showing when we're upset or need to talk.

But real strength isn't about hiding your emotions. Just look at babies—they freely cry when sad and laugh when happy. That's how it should be. Of course, we need to be careful about how we express ourselves in public. But in private, it's important to feel and express what we're going through.

And guess what? AI chatbots can help! They can talk to you with voice, too, not just text. They listen and even give advice—it's almost like chatting with a real person. You can open up to them safely and privately. Pretty cool, right? It's a great way to express yourself and get some insights. Why not give it a shot?

●●●

감정을 억누르지 마.

가끔은 감정을 드러내도 정말 괜찮아. 우리는 자라면서, 특히 사람들 앞에서 감정을 숨기는 법을 배우곤 해. 속상하거나 말해야 할 때 드러내지 않는 걸 강하다고 생각해.

하지만 진짜 강함은 감정을 숨기는 게 아니야. 아기들을 봐. 슬플 땐 마구 울고 행복할 땐 웃잖아. 그게 자연스러운 거야. 물론 사람들 앞에서 자신을 표현하는 데는 주의가 필요해. 하지만 혼자 있을 땐 우리가 겪고 있는 감정을 느끼고 표현하는 게 중요해.

그리고 그거 알아? AI 챗봇이 도와줄 수 있어! 문자로만이 아니라, 목소리를 내며 이야기할 수 있어. 이야기를 들어 주고 조언까지 해 줘. 거의 진짜 사람과 이야기하는 것 같다니까. 안전하게 사적으로 마음을 터놓을 수 있어. 꽤 근사하지? 자신을 표현하고 통찰을 얻는 아주 좋은 방법이야. 한번 해 보는 거 어때?

upset 속상한 | hide 숨기다 | open up to 마음을 터놓다 | insight 통찰

Every Day Is Valuable.

Life really is short, isn't it? We often act like we have all the time in the world, but the truth is, we don't. Each day is precious because once it's gone, it's gone forever. So, think about this when you're deciding how to spend your time.

Let's say a neighbor asks you to hang out, but you don't really want to. It's probably better to say, "No thanks. I have something else on." Remember, you'd be trading a slice of your life for that experience, so ask yourself if it's worth it.

Likewise, if you're about to engage in some mindless entertainment, think twice. Make a list of things you love doing and things you feel are important. Keep this list in mind so that when something comes up, you can compare your options against the list. If they align, great! If not, consider doing something that's more meaningful to you. Your time is valuable, so spend it in ways that bring you joy and fulfillment.

•••

하루하루가 소중해.

삶은 정말 짧아, 안 그래? 우리는 종종 세상의 시간을 다 가진 듯 행동하지만, 사실은 그렇지 않아. 시간은 한번 지나면 영원히 사라져 버리니까, 하루하루가 소중해. 그러니 시간을 어떻게 보낼지 결정할 때 이 점을 고려하도록 해.

이웃 사람이 함께 시간을 보내자고 하는데, 너는 정말 그러고 싶지 않아. 그럴 땐 '아니, 괜찮아요. 다른 일이 있어요'라고 말하는 게 나을지도 몰라. 기억해, 네 삶의 한 조각을 그 경험과 바꾼다면, 그게 그럴 만한 가치가 있는지 스스로에게 물어봐.

마찬가지로, 아무 생각 없이 어떤 활동에 참여하려 할 때도, 한 번 더 생각하도록 해. 하고 싶은 일들과 중요하다고 느껴지는 일들을 목록으로 만들어 봐. 이 목록을 마음에 담아 두고서, 어떤 일이 생겼을 때, 네 선택지를 그 목록과 비교해 볼 수 있어. 그것들이 같은 선상에 있다면 아주 좋아! 그렇지 않다면 너에게 더 의미 있는 일을 하는 걸 고려하도록 해. 네 시간은 소중해, 그러니 기쁨과 만족을 얻는 방식으로 시간을 보내.

precious 소중한 | **a slice** 한 조각 | **engage in** ~에 참여하다

Phase 9

Consolidate and Stabilize

강화하고 안정시키기

"Remember: no matter how good you become,
you'll always have room for improvement."
-from Day 86-

"아무리 잘하게 되어도,
항상 나아질 여지가 있다는 걸 기억해."

One Minute Gratitude Reminder.

Try this out: put an alarm on your phone for a chill time each day. When it buzzes, hit pause on whatever you're doing and just think of one thing that's made you thankful recently. Maybe it's that delicious breakfast you had, a message from a friend, or just the fact that it's drizzling and romantic outside.

This tiny break is like a mini refresh button for your mood. It shifts your focus to the good stuff that's happening around you, and it can make a pretty sweet difference in your day.

It's not just about the huge things, just a quiet minute to acknowledge the good in life. Plus, it's a cool way to make gratitude a regular part of your routine. Give it a whirl—it might just turn your whole day around.

•••

1분 감사 알림

이렇게 한번 해 봐. 매일 쉬는 시간을 정해 휴대 전화에 알람을 맞춰. 진동이 울리면 하던 일을 잠시 멈추고, 최근 감사했던 한 가지를 그냥 떠올려 봐. 맛있게 먹은 아침 식사나 친구에게서 온 메시지, 그저 밖에 이슬비가 내리고 있어 낭만적이라는 사실일 수도 있어.

이 짧은 휴식은 기분을 바꿔 주는 작은 새로 고침 버튼이야. 그건 주변에서 일어나는 좋은 일로 네 초점을 옮겨 주고 네 하루에 꽤 달콤한 변화를 가져다줄 수 있어.

중요한 건 거창한 일만이 아니라, 그저 삶의 좋은 면을 알아보는 조용한 순간이야. 게다가 그건 감사를 일상의 규칙적인 부분으로 만드는 멋진 방식이기도 해. 시도해 봐. 하루 전체가 달라질 수도 있으니까.

buzz 윙윙거리다 | pause 잠시 멈춤 | drizzle 이슬비가 내리다 |
refresh 원기를 회복하다 | give it a whirl 시도하다

The Miracle of Moving.

Feeling overwhelmed with your studies, work, and life's hustle? Instead of just thinking about it, why not try some physical activity? Of course, it's easy to think, "I don't have time for exercise or anything else." But guess what? That type of thinking is exactly what's holding you back in life.

In fact, the busier or more challenging life is, the more you need to move your body and get your heart pumping. Get up from your desk and stretch, go for a short 20-minute walk, or do something else to get your body active. I know it might sound overly simplistic, but there's actual science behind this advice. Physical activity has been shown to be able to totally transform your mood and give you a fresh new perspective on whatever's been worrying you. You'll find problems that initially seemed massive shrink or even disappear. By moving, you're giving yourself a little break to refresh.

So, remember, next time you're feeling stuck or snowed under, just get moving. A little activity can really work wonders.

•••

움직임의 기적

공부와 일, 삶의 분주함에 압도된 느낌이야? 그냥 그렇게 생각하지만 말고 신체 활동을 해 보는 건 어때? 물론 '운동 같은 거 할 시간이 없어'라고 생각하기는 쉬워. 하지만 그거 알아? 바로 그런 식의 생각이 삶에서 너를 가로막는 요인이야.

사실, 삶이 바쁘고 힘들수록 더욱 몸을 움직이고 심장이 뛰게 해야 해. 책상에서 일어나 스트레칭을 하거나, 20분 정도 짧게 산책하거나, 신체를 활동시킬 무언가를 해 봐. 지나치게 단순하게 들릴지도 모르지만, 이 조언 뒤에는 진짜 과학이 숨어 있어. 신체 활동이 기분을 완전히 바꿔 주고, 걱정하던 일에 신선하고 새로운 시각을 준다는 건 입증되었어. 처음엔 거대해 보였던 문제들도 작아지거나 사라지기까지 한다는 걸 발견하게 될 거야. 몸을 움직이는 것으로, 생기를 되찾을 작은 휴식을 자신에게 주는 거야.

그러니 기억해, 다음번에 막막하거나 할 일이 너무 많을 때는 그냥 움직여 봐. 작은 활동 하나가 진짜 기적을 낳을 수 있어.

overly 지나치게, 과도하게 | **simplistic** 지나치게 단순화한 | **massive** 거대한

Day 83

You Can't Really Get Worse.

Remember, if you're putting in the time and effort, there's no such thing as "getting worse." So, let's say you've been practicing hard for a test, but your score is lower than before. Don't stress about it. Improvement isn't a simple straight line; it's more like a dance—two steps forward, one step back. Sometimes you might feel stuck or even like you're going backwards, but that's just part of the dance. The vital thing is to learn from your experiences and become better over time.

So, hold your head up, stay positive, and embrace the process. After all, the important thing isn't where you are now, but where you're headed. And with consistent effort and a positive mindset, you're headed in the right direction!

●●●

정말로 더 나빠질 수는 없어.

시간과 노력을 쏟고 있다면 '더 나빠지는' 일은 없다는 걸 기억해. 시험 준비를 열심히 했는데 점수가 전보다 더 낮게 나왔다고 해 보자. 그래도 스트레스받지 마. 성장은 단순히 직선이 아니거든. 그건 두 걸음 앞으로 갔다 한 걸음 뒤로 가는 춤과 같아. 때로는 멈춰 있다거나 심지어 뒤로 가고 있다고 느껴질 수도 있지만, 그건 춤의 일부분일 뿐이야. 중요한 건 그 경험에서 배우고, 시간이 흐르면서 더 나아지는 거야.

그러니 고개를 들고 긍정적인 마음으로 그 과정을 받아들여. 결국, 지금 어디에 있는지가 아니라 어디로 향하고 있는지가 중요해. 지속적인 노력과 긍정적인 마음가짐으로, 너는 옳은 방향으로 가고 있어!

stress about ~대해 스트레스받다 | **vital** 중대한, 치명적인 | **headed** ~로 가는

Your Life, Your Map.

So, here's the thing, life's full of expectations that other people have for us. It's like everyone's got a map they think we should follow. Maybe it's your parents, teachers, or even your friends. But the deal is, it's your life, your journey. Other people's maps are taken from their own experiences, their own fears, and what they think is best for you.

But when it comes to living your life, you're the one putting one foot in front of the other. So, while it's smart to consider advice from people who care about you, remember your life's your adventure, not theirs. It's okay to explore, make your own choices, and find your own way. Trust me, that's what makes life interesting and uniquely yours. And if you're a parent, don't insist that your kids follow your map.

●●●

너의 삶, 너의 지도

삶은 다른 사람들이 우리에게 하는 기대로 가득해. 모든 사람이 우리가 따라야 한다고 생각하는 지도를 가지고 있는 것 같아. 그 사람들은 부모님이나 선생님, 친구일 수도 있어. 하지만 중요한 건 그게 네 삶이고 여정이라는 거야. 다른 사람들은 그들만의 경험, 두려움, 그들이 너에게 가장 좋다고 생각하는 것들로 지도를 그려.

하지만 네 삶을 사는 것에 관한 한, 한 발 한 발 나아가는 사람은 바로 너야. 너를 염려하는 사람들의 조언을 고려하는 건 현명한 일이지만, 네 삶은 그들의 것이 아니라 네 모험이라는 걸 기억해. 탐색하고, 스스로 결정하고, 스스로 길을 찾는 건 괜찮아. 날 믿어, 그게 바로 삶을 흥미롭게 너만의 것으로 만드는 거야. 그리고 네가 부모라면, 자녀가 네 지도를 따르도록 강요하지는 마.

expectation 기대 | consider 고려하다, 숙고하다 | insist 강요하다, 고집하다

Don't Try to "Fix" Each Other.

You know what the secret sauce to a happy relationship is? It's mutual respect, not this urge to "fix" each other. I get it; after being with someone for a while, those once-adorable quirks might start to feel like annoying habits. But hold on— weren't those differences part of what sparked your interest in the first place? Let's be real, if you were dating (or married) to a copy of yourself, you'd be bored out of your mind.

So, let's drop this whole "change them" mission, shall we? There's this killer quote I love: "If two people agree on everything, one of those people isn't necessary." Think about it. Differences add flavor to life and your relationship. Appreciate them, and you'll see just how much they enrich the love you share.

•••

서로를 '고치려' 하지 마.

행복한 관계의 비밀 양념이 뭔지 알아? 그건 서로를 '고치려는' 욕구가 아니라, 서로에 대한 존중이야. 나도 이해해. 누군가와 얼마간 함께하다 보면 한때는 사랑스러웠던 별난 점이 짜증 나는 습관처럼 느껴지기 시작할 수도 있어. 그런데 잠깐, 그 차이들이 처음에 네 관심을 끈 부분 아냐? 솔직히 말해, 네가 네 복사본과 사귄다면 (혹은 결혼한다면) 못 견디게 지루할 거야.

그러니 '그들을 바꾸는' 임무는 이제 내려놓자, 응? 내가 정말 좋아하는 멋진 인용구가 있어. '두 사람이 모든 것에 동의한다면, 둘 중 하나는 필요치 않다.' 생각해 봐. 다름은 삶과 관계에 풍미를 더해 줘. 차이를 인정하면, 네가 나누는 사랑이 얼마나 풍요로워지는지 알게 될 거야.

urge 욕구, 충동 | adorable 사랑스러운 |
quirk 별난 점 | quote 인용구 | enrich 풍요롭게 하다

Day 86

Welcome a Stronger Version of Yourself.

I'm sure you know growing's a bit like a journey, right? And on this journey, feedback's your compass. Sure, it feels great to hear the good stuff, but the real gold is in the advice that helps you grow. So, regularly touch base with folks you trust—teachers, friends, or mentors—and ask them for the honest truth. What could you do better? How can you stretch yourself a bit more?

It's not about being tough on yourself; it's about getting the tools to build a stronger, smarter you. Think of criticism as your personal trainer for life skills, making you more resilient and adaptable.

Remember: no matter how good you become, you'll always have room for improvement. Proactively take criticism on board and welcome a stronger version of yourself.

●●●

자신의 더 강한 버전을 환영해 줘.

성장이 여정과 비슷하다는 건 너도 알 거야, 그치? 그리고 이 여정에서 피드백은 나침반이야. 물론, 좋은 말을 듣는 건 기분 좋지만, 진짜 보물은 성장을 돕는 조언 속에 있어. 그러니 신뢰하는 사람들인 선생님이나 친구, 멘토와 정기적으로 연락하고 솔직한 의견을 물어봐. 네가 뭘 더 잘할 수 있을까? 어떻게 조금 더 성장할 수 있을까?

중요한 건 자신을 몰아붙이는 게 아니라, 더 강하고 똑똑한 자신을 만드는 도구를 갖추는 거야. 비판이 삶의 기술을 가르쳐 주는 개인 트레이너라고 생각해 봐. 너를 더 회복력 있고 유연하게 만들어 줄 테니까.

아무리 잘하게 되어도, 항상 나아질 여지가 있다는 걸 기억해. 먼저 나서서 비판을 받아들이고 자신의 더 강한 버전을 환영해 줘.

compass 나침반 | **mentor** 멘토 | **proactively** 상황을 앞서서 주도하는

You Have the Right to Choose to Be Happy.

Sometimes life can get totally crazy with work and an endless list of things to do. It feels like you're almost drowning in it, right? No matter how busy we get, it's super important to stay calm and cool.

Don't start your day telling yourself it's going to be tough. Instead, change your mood—like listening to your favorite song or enjoying a nice drink—and tell yourself, "Okay, today might be busy and tiring, but it's still going to be a great day." Doing this and staying relaxed makes everything go smoother.

It's all about accepting things as they are without letting the outside world bother you. Even on busy or exhausting days, you can easily handle it. Remember, choosing to be happy is totally up to you. You've got this!

●●●

넌 행복을 선택할 권리가 있어.

삶이 직장 일과 끝없이 해야 할 일들로 완전히 정신없어질 때가 있어. 마치 그 속에 빠져 허우적대는 듯한 기분이야, 그렇지? 하지만 아무리 바빠도, 침착과 냉정을 유지하는 건 굉장히 중요해.

스스로 힘들 거라고 말하며 하루를 시작하지 마. 대신, 좋아하는 노래를 듣거나 맛있는 음료를 즐기며 기분을 바꾸고 스스로에게 '좋아, 오늘 바쁘고 피곤할 수도 있지만, 그래도 여전히 멋진 하루가 될 거야'라고 말해 봐. 이렇게 하며 긴장을 풀면 모든 게 더 매끄럽게 흘러가.

바깥세상이 너를 귀찮게 하도록 두지 말고 모든 걸 있는 그대로 받아들여. 그러면 바쁘고 지치는 날에도 쉽게 대처할 수 있어. 기억해, 행복을 선택하는 건 완전히 너에게 달렸어. 넌 할 수 있어!

endless 끝없는 | drown 익사시키다 | bother 귀찮게 하다 | exhausting 지치는

Complaining About Lacking Talent Is Just an Excuse to Be Lazy.

Many of us have a "fixed mindset," in which we believe our lack of inborn talent limits us and prevents improvement. However, studies have shown that adopting a "growth mindset" can lead to development through hard work and seeing failures as opportunities for growth.

Instead of focusing on innate talents, we should work hard to improve ourselves, even if we're not naturally gifted. Complaining about lacking intelligence or talent is just an excuse to be lazy.

Take math as an example. In elementary school, many people who can't keep up with the class are labeled as "terrible at math." But in reality, everyone has the potential for mathematical ability. Numerous studies have shown that everybody has a "math brain" and that math skills can be acquired through learning and practice. And this growth mindset applies to developing other abilities as well. Isn't that exciting?

•••

재능이 없다는 불평은 그저 게으름을 피우려는 핑계일 뿐이야.

많은 사람이 '고정형 사고방식', 즉 타고난 재능의 부족이 우리 한계를 정하고 발전을 방해한다는 믿음을 가지고 있어. 하지만 연구는 '성장형 사고방식'을 택하면 노력과 실패를 성장의 기회로 보는 눈을 통해 발전할 수 있다는 사실을 보여 줘.

비록 우리가 선천적으로 타고나지 않았어도, 타고난 재능에 초점을 맞추는 대신, 스스로 나아지도록 열심히 노력해야 해. 지능이나 재능이 부족하다고 불평하는 건 그저 게으름을 피우려는 핑계일 뿐이야.

수학을 예로 들어 보자. 초등학교 때 수업을 따라가지 못하는 많은 아이에게 '수학에 형편없다'라는 꼬리표가 붙어. 하지만 실제로 수학 능력은 누구에게나 잠재되어 있어. 수많은 연구에 따르면 모든 사람이 '수학 두뇌'를 갖고 있고 수학 실력은 학습과 연습을 통해 얻을 수 있다고 해. 그리고 이 성장형 사고방식은 다른 능력들을 발전시키는 데도 적용할 수 있어. 신나지 않아?

inborn talent 타고난 재능 | innate 타고난 | numerous 수많은 | acquire 얻다

Accept Yourself, Warts and All.

Self-acceptance is like giving yourself a big hug, recognizing that you're awesome just the way you are. It's about loving and embracing every part of you, even the warts, the bits you're not so happy about.

Here's a simple idea to practice self-acceptance: every day, stand in front of the mirror and say one thing you like about yourself. It could be anything—maybe your sense of humor or how you helped a friend. For instance, if you did a good job in completing your homework or just made a killer omelet, acknowledge it. Say, "Hey, I did that, and I did it really well." This is like giving yourself a pat on the back regularly.

It boosts your confidence and helps you see yourself in a positive light. Remember, the more you appreciate yourself, the brighter your world becomes.

●●●

결점도 있는 그대로, 자신을 받아들여.

자기 수용은 자신을 꼭 안아 주면서, 자신이 있는 그대로 멋지다는 사실을 알아봐 주는 것과 같아. 그다지 좋게 느끼지 않는 부분, 결점까지도, 자신의 모든 부분을 사랑하고 안아 주는 거야.

자기 수용을 연습하는 간단한 방법이 하나 있어. 매일, 거울 앞에 서서 자신에 대해 좋아하는 점을 한 가지 말해 보는 거야. 어떤 거라도 좋아. 유머 감각이나 친구를 도와준 일도 괜찮아. 예를 들어, 숙제를 잘 마쳤거나 죽여 주는 오믈렛을 만들었다면 그걸 인정해 줘. '그래, 난 그걸 해냈고, 정말 잘했어'라고 말해 줘. 마치 자신을 꾸준히 칭찬해 주는 것과 같아.

이 방법은 자신감을 높여 주고, 긍정적인 시선으로 자신을 보도록 도와줄 거야. 기억해, 자신을 인정할수록 네 세상은 더 밝아지리라는 걸.

killer 죽여 주는 것 | acknowledge 인정하다 | a pat on the back 칭찬

Forgiveness Is for You.

There's this idea that time can heal everything, and in a way, it's true. When someone does something that hurts us, we might feel really upset at first. But as time passes, we sometimes find those hard feelings fading away.

Yet, holding onto anger and resentment doesn't change what happened; it only makes it harder to forgive. Research shows these feelings can even mess with your health, like harming the immune system and triggering emotional gastrointestinal diseases, among other issues. So, what's the point in keeping them around?

Here's a thought: try forgiving everyone for everything, and do it now, not years later. It sounds tough, I know, but it's really for you, not them. Forgiving is like setting yourself free from carrying around all that heavy stuff. It's not about saying what they did was okay. It's about giving yourself the gift of moving on and finding happiness. When you let go of grudges, you make room for peace in your heart. And that's a pretty amazing feeling.

●●●

용서는 널 위한 거야.

시간이 모든 걸 치유해 줄 수 있다는 개념이 있고, 그건 어느 정도는 사실이야. 누군가에게 상처받았을 때, 처음엔 정말 속상할지도 몰라. 하지만 시간이 지나면서, 때로 그 힘든 감정이 점점 희미해지는 걸 발견하게 되기도 해.

하지만 분노와 원망은 붙잡고 있어 봤자 이미 일어난 일을 바꾸지는 못해. 용서하기를 더 어렵게 할 뿐이야. 연구에 따르면 이런 감정이 건강도 해칠 수 있다고 해. 다른 문제 중에서도 특히, 면역 체계에 해를 끼치고 감정적 요인에 의한 소화기 질환을 유발해. 그러니 그런 감정을 간직해 봐야 무슨 의미가 있어?

제안 하나 할게. 모든 사람의 모든 일을 용서하도록 해. 지금 해, 몇 년 후가 아니라. 어렵게 들리는 거 알아, 하지만 정말로 너를 위해서야. 용서는 그 무거운 짐을 지고 다니는 데서 자신을 해방해 주는 거야. 그들이 한 일이 괜찮다는 말이 아니야. 중요한 건 스스로가 앞으로 나아가며 행복을 찾는 선물을 주는 거지. 원한을 떠나보내면 마음속에 평화가 들어올 공간이 생겨. 그리고 그건 꽤 멋진 기분이야.

fade 희미해지다 | **immune system** 면역 체계 | **trigger** 유발하다 | **grudge** 원한

Phase

10

Continually
Go Beyond

계속해서 넘어서

"So, in the face of difficulties, remember,
it's not about the strength of your punch
but the spirit that drives it."
-from Day 96-

"그러니 어려움에 직면하면, 주먹의 힘이 아니라,
그 주먹을 움직이는 정신이 중요하다는 걸 기억해."

Gratitude Journaling for a Better Tomorrow.

Let me ask you a question: have you ever thought about starting a gratitude journal? It's a simple but powerful way to shift your focus and boost your mood. All you need to do is write down between three and five things you're thankful for each day. They can be big or small—from a beautiful sunset to a tasty snack or a nice message from a friend.

Taking the time to reflect on the positive aspects of your life can really change your perspective and make you feel happier overall. It's like training your mind to look for the good stuff, and if you really think about it, there's always something good to be found.

Do this exercise before going to bed every night, and your subconscious mind will keep thinking about how great your life is. Then, you'll have a much better day the next day. Give it a try and see how it makes a difference in your life!

더 나은 내일을 위한 감사 일기

질문 하나 할게. 감사 일기를 써 볼 생각, 해 본 적 있어? 감사 일기는 너의 초점을 바꾸고 기분을 북돋아 줄 단순하지만 강력한 방법이야. 네가 해야 하는 건, 매일 감사한 일을 세 가지에서 다섯 가지 적는 게 다야. 크든 작든, 아름다운 노을부터 맛있는 간식까지, 혹은 친구에게서 온 기분 좋은 메시지도 괜찮아.

삶의 긍정적인 면을 되돌아보는 시간을 가지면, 보는 시각이 정말로 달라지고 전반적으로 더 행복해져. 마음이 좋은 것을 찾아내도록 훈련하는 일과 같아. 그리고 곰곰이 생각해 보면, 항상 감사할 무언가는 있기 마련이야.

매일 밤, 잠들기 전에 이 연습을 해 봐. 네 삶이 얼마나 대단한지에 대해 네 잠재의식이 계속 생각할 거야. 그러면 다음 날은 훨씬 더 좋은 하루가 될 거야. 한번 해 보고, 삶이 어떻게 달라지는지 지켜봐.

boost 북돋우다 | reflect on 되돌아보다 |
aspect 측면 | subconscious mind 잠재의식

Focus on What You Can Control.

Many things in life are completely out of your hands. Focus on what you can control. It's like steering your own ship in the ocean of life. It's putting your energy where it really counts and can make a difference, instead of worrying about the waves you can't calm.

Try this: make a list of things that worry you and divide them into two categories—things you can control and things you can't. For example, you can't control the traffic on an important day, but you can control how early you leave. Likewise, you can't control the outcome in the university admissions process, but you can control the amount of effort you make before applying to college.

Whenever you find yourself anxious because of stress, look at your list and ask, "Is this something I can change?" If yes, work on it; if not, let it be. This helps you focus on the actions that truly matter and teaches you to let go of unnecessary worries. Remember, where focus goes, energy flows. Keep steering your ship wisely!

● ● ●

통제할 수 있는 것에 집중해.

삶의 많은 것이 완전히 네 능력 밖의 일이야. 그러니 통제할 수 있는 것에 집중하도록 해. 삶이라는 바다에서 자기 배를 조종하는 거나 마찬가지야. 가라앉힐 수 없는 파도를 걱정하는 대신, 가치가 있고 차이를 만들 수 있는 곳에 에너지를 쏟는 거야.

이렇게 한번 해 봐. 걱정스러운 일들을 목록으로 만들고 통제할 수 있는 것과 없는 것, 두 종류로 나눠 봐. 예를 들어, 중요한 날에 교통량을 통제할 수는 없지만, 얼마나 일찍 나갈지는 정할 수 있어. 마찬가지로, 대학 입학 과정에서 결과를 통제할 순 없지만, 대학에 지원하기 전 얼마나 노력할지는 선택할 수 있어.

스트레스 때문에 불안해질 때마다, 목록을 보고 '내가 바꿀 수 있는 걸까?' 하고 물어봐. 맞다면 노력해 보고, 아니라면 그냥 둬. 이건 정말로 중요한 행동에 집중하는 걸 도와주고 불필요한 걱정을 내려놓는 법을 가르쳐 줘. 기억해, 초점이 향하는 곳으로 에너지가 흐른다는 걸. 배를 계속 현명하게 조종하는 거야!

out of your hands 능력 밖인 | steer 조종하다 |
category 종류 | outcome 결과

It Takes Just 15 Minutes.

All you can do is all you can do, but trust me, all you can do is enough. If you're already giving it your all, don't beat yourself up for not doing more.

If, however, you find yourself slacking off, take action now. Even something as simple as setting a timer for 15 minutes (or 10, or even 5) can make a world of difference. As long as it feels manageable, go for it.

Here's an idea: spend 15 minutes, right now if possible, either copying or reading out the passages in this book. If you haven't started doing it yet, it'll be a small step that will kickstart your learning again. And if you're up for it, increase the time by another 15 minutes, and keep doing that until you need to take a break. The key is consistency. Use this 15-minute technique daily, and before you know it, you'll be back on track with your learning journey.

● ● ●

딱 15분이면 충분해.

네가 할 수 있는 모든 게 네가 할 수 있는 모든 거야. 하지만 날 믿어, 네가 할 수 있는 모든 걸로 충분해. 이미 최선을 다하고 있다면, 더 하지 못했다고 자책하지 마.

하지만 자신이 게으름을 피우고 있다고 생각한다면, 지금 당장 행동해. 15분 (아니면 10분, 아니면 5분이라도) 타이머를 맞추는 것처럼 간단한 일도 엄청난 차이를 만들 수 있어. 감당할 수 있는 한, 해 봐.

아이디어가 하나 있어. 가능하다면 지금 당장 15분을 할애해서 이 책의 구절들을 베껴 쓰거나 소리 내어 읽어 봐. 아직 시작하지 않았다면 배움을 다시 시작하게 해 줄 작은 한 걸음이 될 거야. 그리고 괜찮다면, 시간을 15분 늘리고 쉬어야 할 때까지 계속해 봐. 핵심은 꾸준함이야. 이 15분 기술을 매일 활용하다 보면, 어느새 배움의 여정에 정상 궤도로 돌아올 거야.

slack off 게으름 피우다 | manageable 감당할 수 있는 |
consistency 일관성, 꾸준함

The Past Doesn't Have to Equal the Future.

I've got some great news! Your past doesn't have to define your future, not one bit. Yeah, you might have messed up before, but guess what? Most of the super successful people you hear about started with nothing. They were not born rich—they earned it. And most of them messed up lots before they hit it big. Don't be fooled into thinking they just got lucky; they worked really hard for years to achieve what they now have.

So, don't get stuck on past results (like poor grades, going to a poorly ranked college, being in a low position at work, etc.) thinking that's all you can do. Your future potential is limitless. So, aim high, aim for what you really want, not just what you think you can get based on your past. Trust me, you'll be glad you did.

•••

과거가 미래와 같을 필요는 없어.

아주 좋은 소식이 있어! 네 과거가 미래를 규정지을 필요는 전혀 없다는 거야. 그래, 예전에 망친 적이 있을 수도 있지, 하지만 그거 알아? 네가 아는 엄청나게 성공한 사람들 대부분 아무것도 없이 시작했어. 그들은 부자로 태어나지 않았어, 얻어 낸 거지. 그들 대부분 성공하기 전에 수없이 실패했어. 그저 운이 좋았다는 생각에 속지 마. 그들은 수년간 지금 가진 걸 이루려고 정말 열심히 노력했으니까.

그러니 과거의 결과(나쁜 성적, 등급이 낮은 대학에 간 것, 직장에서 낮은 직급에 있는 것 등)에 갇혀, 그게 네가 할 수 있는 전부라고 생각하지는 마. 미래의 가능성은 무궁무진해. 그러니, 높은 곳을 겨냥해. 과거에 근거해서 할 수 있다고 생각하는 것만이 아니라, 네가 정말로 원하는 걸 목표로 삼아. 날 믿어, 그렇게 한 걸 나중에 기뻐할 테니까.

define 규정하다, 정의하다 | not one bit 전혀 | be fooled 속다

Every Day Beats Special Days.

We often think of romance as special days of celebration and special dates. We think that the perfect confession, the perfect proposal, or the perfect wedding day are the most important parts of a relationship. But guess what? As important as these special days are, they are nowhere near as important as the daily kindnesses that you show each other. If you are kind to each other all the time, every day can be as sweet as your honeymoon.

Right now, think about several things that you could do to make your relationship a little bit more special. Perhaps, you could send a romantic text to your other half, give them a drink they like without being asked, or buy them something small but unexpected. It really doesn't have to be a big thing. Remember, much of the time, it's the thought that counts, not the expense.

•••

매일이 특별한 날을 이겨.

우리는 종종 연애를 특별한 기념일과 특별한 데이트로 생각해. 완벽한 고백, 완벽한 청혼, 완벽한 결혼식이 관계에서 가장 중요한 부분이라고 생각하지. 하지만 그거 알아? 이런 특별한 날들도 중요하지만, 서로에게 매일 보여 주는 상냥함의 중요함에는 미치지 않는다는 걸. 항상 서로에게 친절하면 하루하루가 신혼여행만큼 달콤해질 수 있어.

지금 당장 관계를 조금 더 특별하게 만들 수 있는 몇 가지를 생각해 봐. 가령, 연인에게 낭만적인 문자를 보내거나, 그들이 요청하진 않았지만 좋아할 음료를 건네거나, 작지만 예상치 못한 선물을 사 주는 것도 좋아. 거창할 필요 없어. 많은 경우, 중요한 건 돈이 아니라 마음이란 걸 기억해.

confession 고백 | proposal 청혼 |
nowhere near 미치지 않는, 거리가 먼 | expense 비용

The Spirit to Keep Punching.

Grit is like being in a boxing ring with life. It's not always about how hard you can hit, but how many hits you can take and keep moving forward. It's about not letting a knockdown turn into a knockout.

Every challenge you face is going to throw punches at you. Some will be soft, easy to dodge, while others might hit hard, knocking you down. But having grit means even if you get knocked down, you never stay down. You keep punching, not because you're unafraid or unharmed, but because you're determined.

You know that with each punch you throw back, you're one step closer to winning your fight, achieving your goals. So, in the face of difficulties, remember, it's not about the strength of your punch but the spirit that drives it. Keep punching, keep moving, and you'll see, nothing can keep you down for long.

•••

계속 싸우는 정신

근성은 삶과 함께 복싱 링에 있는 것과 같아. 중요한 건 얼마나 세게 칠 수 있는지가 아니라 얼마나 많은 타격을 견디고 계속 앞으로 나아갈 수 있는지야. 잠깐의 좌절이 포기가 되지 않도록 하는 거지.

네가 직면한 모든 도전이 네게 주먹을 날릴 거야. 몇몇은 약하고 피하기 쉽겠지만, 다른 몇몇은 강하게 꽂혀서 너를 나가떨어지게 할지도 몰라. 하지만 근성이 있다는 건 나가떨어져도 쓰러진 채로 있지 않는다는 거야. 계속 쳐, 두렵지 않거나 다치지 않아서가 아니라, 그렇게 하기로 결정했으니까.

알다시피, 네가 받아칠 때마다 너는 그 싸움에 승리하는 데, 목표를 이루는 데 한 걸음 더 가까워져. 그러니 어려움에 직면하면, 주먹의 힘이 아니라, 그 주먹을 움직이는 정신이 중요하다는 걸 기억해. 계속 치고, 계속 움직여, 그러면 그 무엇도 너를 계속 쓰러져 있게 할 수 없다는 걸 알게 될 거야.

boxing ring 복싱 링 | knockdown 녹다운, 잠시 쓰러짐 |
knockout 녹아웃, 완전히 쓰러져 다시 일어나지 못함(KO) | dodge 재빨리 피하다

The Fewer Rules You Have, the Happier You'll Be.

You know how we sometimes trap ourselves with lots of "I don't likes" and "I can't accepts"? Things like, "I don't like this," "I can't accept that," or insisting "It has to be this way." The more we do this, the more the world seems to fight back, and it can make us feel pretty down.

But here's a cool tip: try to start letting go of these self-imposed rules. For instance, if you believe people must answer you in a certain way, you need to understand that they might have different rules and that you can't really force others to follow your rules. Then, let go of the rule and be willing to accept people as they really are. You might be surprised! When you start accepting things you thought you couldn't, life gets simpler.

Open your heart and drop those stubborn views. The fewer rules you set for yourself and others, the happier you'll be.

●●●

규칙이 적으면 적을수록 더 행복해질 거야.

우리가 때로 많은 '싫어'와 '받아들일 수 없어'에 어떻게 자신을 가두는지 알아? '이거 싫어', '그거 받아들일 수 없어' 같은 거나 '꼭 이렇게 해야 해'라며 고집하는 거 말이야. 우리가 이렇게 하면 할수록 세상은 더 거세게 맞서는 것 같고, 그건 우리를 꽤 우울하게 해.

하지만 여기 근사한 팁이 있어. 스스로 만든 이런 규칙들을 내려놓기 시작해 봐. 예를 들어, 사람들이 어떤 특정한 방식으로 대답해야 한다고 믿는다면, 그들에게는 다른 규칙이 있을 수도 있고, 다른 사람들에게 너의 규칙을 강요할 수 없다는 걸 이해해야 해. 그다음에는 그 규칙을 내려놓고 사람들을 있는 그대로의 모습으로 기꺼이 받아들여 봐. 놀랄지도 몰라! 받아들일 수 없다고 생각했던 것들을 받아들이기 시작할 때, 삶은 더 단순해지거든.

마음을 열고 그 고집스러운 생각을 내려놔. 자신과 다른 이들에게 정해 놓은 규칙이 적으면 적을수록 너는 더 행복해질 거야.

trap 가두다 | **self-imposed rule** 스스로 만든 규칙 | **stubborn** 완고한, 고집 센

You're Going to Go off Course.

Here's a fun fact: when you're on a plane, you're actually off course about 95% of the time! Crazy, right? But the pilot keeps adjusting, and, like magic, you arrive at your destination.

The same goes for life. You're going to go off course; that's a given. Don't try to never mess up or even avoid the same mistakes forever. No one's that perfect!

What's important is catching those mistakes and learning how to get back on target. The name of the game is reducing how often you go off track, not beating yourself up when you do. So, if you find yourself going the wrong way, just remember it's all part of the journey. Course correct, keep moving, and you'll still reach your destination.

●●●

너는 항로를 벗어날 거야.

재미있는 사실이 있어. 비행기를 타고 있을 때, 실제로 타고 있는 95%의 비행시간 동안 항로를 벗어나 있다는 거야. 놀랍지? 하지만 조종사는 계속 방향을 조정하고, 순식간에 목적지에 도착해.

인생도 마찬가지야. 너는 항로를 벗어날 거야. 그건 정해진 일이야. 절대 망치지 않겠다거나, 심지어 같은 실수를 영원히 피하겠다는 시도는 하지도 마. 그렇게 완벽한 사람은 없어!

중요한 건 그 실수를 잡아내고 목표로 돌아갈 방법을 배우는 거야. 핵심은 경로를 이탈할 때마다 자책하는 게 아니라, 이탈하는 횟수를 줄이는 거야. 그러니 잘못된 길로 가고 있다면, 그게 모두 여정의 일부란 걸 기억해. 항로를 바로잡고, 계속 나아가면, 결국 목적지에 다다를 테니까.

off course 항로에서 벗어나 | back on target 표적으로 돌아가는 | go off track 경로를 이탈하다

The Art of Doing Nothing.

Did you know it's actually fine to just do nothing once in a while? If you think taking a break is only for lazy people, it's time to change that mindset.

Like breathing, there's a rhythm to work and relaxation—inhale is work, exhale is rest, and both are super important. Constantly working without a break is like holding your breath for too long—eventually, you have to breathe out. Pushing yourself non-stop can lead to burnout or even getting sick. Your body's telling you, "I need some downtime." So, if you want to relax and watch part of a TV series, go for a stroll, get a really good night's sleep, or even take a few days off, that's totally okay. It's your way of exhaling.

But remember, balance is key. It's not about doing nothing or being busy all the time, but about finding the right mix of activity and relaxation, say 70% work and 30% relaxation. Stay balanced, and you'll feel so much better!

●●●

아무것도 하지 않는 기술

가끔은 그냥 아무것도 하지 않아도 괜찮다는 사실, 알고 있었어? 쉬는 게 게으른 사람만 하는 일이라고 생각한다면, 이제 그 마음가짐을 바꿔야 할 때야.

숨 쉬는 것처럼 일과 휴식에도 리듬이 있어. 들숨은 일이고 날숨을 휴식이라서, 둘 다 굉장히 중요해. 쉬지 않고 끊임없이 일하는 건 숨을 너무 오래 참고 있는 거나 다름없어. 언젠가는 숨을 내쉬어야 해. 자신을 멈추지 않고 밀어붙이다 보면 번아웃이 오거나 몸이 아플 수도 있어. 몸이 '휴식이 필요해'라고 말하고 있는 거야. 그러니 쉬면서 드라마를 보거나, 산책하러 가거나, 푹 자거나, 며칠간 쭉 쉬고 싶다면, 그래도 정말 괜찮아. 그건 숨을 내쉬는 너만의 방식이니까.

하지만 균형이 핵심이란 걸 기억해. 중요한 건 아무것도 하지 않거나 늘 바쁜 게 아니라, 일 70%, 휴식 30% 정도로, 활동과 휴식의 적절한 조화를 찾는 거야. 균형을 잡으면 기분이 훨씬 더 좋아질걸!

음원 바로 듣기

It's Never Too Late.

Did you know that it's never too late to pick up something new or make a change? Well, it's a little-known truth.

Life's flexible. Suppose you've been thinking about getting fit but feel like you've missed the boat. Not at all! You can start small. For example, try a 10-minute home workout, take a brisk walk around your neighborhood, or even join a beginner's Pilates class. These little steps can kickstart your fitness journey.

It's all about taking that first step and enjoying the process. Every small effort counts and adds up to big changes over time. The same goes for any new skill or hobby. Want to learn cooking? Start with simple recipes. Dreaming of painting? Begin with basic techniques.

It's your journey, and it's never too late to embark on it. Dive in, explore, and most importantly, have fun with it. You've got this!

●●●

결코 너무 늦은 때란 없어.

새로운 걸 배우거나 변화하기에 결코 너무 늦은 때란 없다는 걸 알고 있었어? 잘 알려지지 않은 진실이야.

삶은 유연해. 운동을 시작하려고 생각해 왔지만, 이미 너무 늦은 것 같은 기분이라고 가정해 보자. 전혀 늦지 않았어! 작은 것부터 시작하면 돼. 예를 들어 10분 홈 트레이닝을 해 보거나, 동네를 빠르게 걷거나, 초급 필라테스 수업에 들어가 봐. 이런 작은 걸음들이 체력 단련이라는 여정에 시동을 걸 수 있어.

첫걸음을 내딛고 그 과정을 즐기는 게 중요해. 작은 노력 하나하나가 가치 있고, 시간이 흐르면서 큰 변화로 이어져. 새로운 기술이나 취미도 마찬가지야. 요리를 배우고 싶어? 간단한 레시피부터 시작해. 그림을 그리고 싶어? 기본적인 기법부터 시작해 봐.

그건 너만의 여정이고, 시작하기에 늦은 때란 없어. 여정에 뛰어들고 탐험하며 무엇보다 중요한 건 그걸 즐기는 거야. 넌 할 수 있어!

원어민 강사가 집필한 가장 진솔하고 긍정적인 영어 가이드북!

인생에서 가장 중요한 10가지 주제를 10일 주기로 차례로 다루며, 독자에게 영감을 불어넣고 잠재력을 깨워 활력을 되찾게 해 줍니다. **매일 10분만 따라 쓰면 놀라운 변화가 시작됩니다.**

· 25년 경력의 미국 대학(원) 입시·유학 시험 전문 원어민 강사가 집필한
자연스럽고 현실적인 구어체 영어

원어민이 일상에서 실제로 사용하는 표현들로 구성되어 있어,
필사 과정만으로도 자연스럽게 원어민식 영어에 가까워질 수 있습니다.

· 원어민 저자의 음성을 듣고, 따라 읽고, 필사하는 삼중 학습 효과!

자연스러운 문장 구조·어휘·리듬·억양을 무의식적으로 체득할 수 있습니다.

· 매일 새로운 주제와 관점을 제공하는 10일 순환 학습법!

감사, 역경 극복, 배움, 목표와 꿈, 사랑, 근성, 행복, 성장, 자기 돌봄, 인생 철학 등,
10가지 주제가 간격 반복 학습(spaced repetition) 원리에 따라 순환되어,
기억에 강하게 남고 기존 지식과 자연스럽게 연결됩니다.

· 영어 실력과 삶의 지혜를 동시에 성장시키는 자기계발형 영어 학습서

영어 문법과 어휘력 향상은 물론, 각 글에 담긴 인생 메시지까지 내면화할 수 있습니다.

값 16,800원
ISBN 979-11-7550-554-4 13740